FUNNY
YOU
SHOULD
ASK...
AGAIN

MORE OF YOUR QUESTIONS ANSWERED BY THE QI ELVES

WITH A FOREWORD BY ZOE BALL

faber

First published in 2021
by Faber & Faber Ltd
Bloomsbury House
74–77 Great Russell Street
London WC1B 3DA
Published in the USA in 2021

Illustrations by Emily Jupitus
Design by Chris Shamwana
Typeset by Ian Bahrami
Printed and bound in England by CPI Group (UK) Ltd,
Croydon CR0 4YY

A CIP record for this book
is available from the British Library

ISBN 978–0–571–37329–1

2 4 6 8 10 9 7 5 3 1

Contents

Foreword
Zoe Ball ponders and wonders
with the QI Elves

. . . .

Zoe: This book was inspired by a segment on my BBC Radio 2 show called the 'Why Workshop'. Once a week, I invite the British people to pose their most brain-befuddling questions to the unbefuddlable brains of the QI Elves. These pages contain the best of those questions and their brilliantly satisfying answers, along with endless tangents and extraordinary facts.

Having read the book and marvelled at their answers, I decided it was only fair to let the authors ask a few questions of their own. Elves, fire away!

QI Elves: Every Wednesday we invade your airwaves to expound on long johns (p. 169), sideburns (p. 94), stinging nettles (p. 171), fig wasps (p. 172), Bubble Wrap (p. 89) or whatever other subjects come our way that week. Why do you let us keep doing it?

Zoe: We love it. In the studio we think of you all as rock stars and get giddy and excited when you come in. We even have a chart of our favourites, in terms of cleverness, hilariousness, best on a night out, handsomeness –

QI Elves: We have to see that chart.

Zoe: We'll never show you – it'd be like revealing who your favourite child is!

But, really, the thing you all share, which comes across in this book, is that killer combination of smart and funny. It's like the great teacher everyone remembers from school who always made you laugh and told you fascinating things, usually completely unrelated to what they were supposed to be teaching you. You're learning, but it's never boring, and it's never a lecture; it's always light and non-patronising.

QI Elves: Well, we're in no position to patronise anyone, because we're starting from the same point as everyone else, which is one of almost total ignorance. We're strong believers in the idea that you'll only be wise once you accept that you know nothing – the Socratic paradox (although technically that isn't what Socrates said, but that's a discussion for another time). We love admitting we don't know something, because then we get the joy of learning and sharing it. Imagine how bleak life would be if you suddenly realised you had nothing left to learn.

Quite a lot of what you do pick up in the book might seem pointless or trivial. In these serious times, is there really a place for such silliness as whether dogs can tell the time (p. 75) or what a dinosaur's bottom looked like (p. 143)?

Zoe: Definitely. Now more than ever it's important because we need an escape. The pandemic has dominated everyone's lives and thoughts these past couple of years and taken a terrible toll on so many people. Sometimes a bit of good old-fashioned silliness can take that load off for a moment. And everything in here is a reminder that there's still a lot to love about the world, whether it's that ants actually count the number of steps they do each day (p. 4), or that you really can crack a safe with a stethoscope (p. 154), or that there's a light in California that's been left on for 120 years (p. 81).

I know people appreciate it because when I'm out and about, in the supermarket or on the street, people stop me and quote amazing answers and facts that they've learnt from you guys.

QI Elves: Ah, sorry about that. People love nothing more than to share an interesting fact, when sometimes you were really just hoping to dash out and buy some coriander.

Okay, so if you were going to buy this book for one person, who would it be?

Zoe: That's impossible. I can't choose just one person. I'd be tempted to say my dad, but he knows so much that he'd have more to say on every subject in here, and you'd never get away. I bought last year's edition for everyone in my family. In my household we have a copy in the downstairs loo, and I always check when I go in to see if the order of the books that I keep in there has changed. It makes me happy when I see it back on top again.

I've got lots of nieces and nephews – there are loads of Balls – so I'll get it for all of them. All of us love facts, so it's the perfect conversation-starter; you end up talking about everything you read in here.

QI Elves: Well done. That was a trick question, and you escaped the *QI* klaxon. Obviously, you shouldn't buy this for just one person; you should buy it for everyone you know. Because *all* humans have a childlike curiosity. This is what makes us human – we're more immature than other mammals. The technical word is 'neoteny', which is the tendency to retain youthful features, even in adulthood. Compared to other apes, we have shorter arms, flatter faces, a bigger brain-to-body-size ratio, and we're mostly hairless. These are all childish traits, which apes lose as they age, but we don't. And to top it all off, we stay curious throughout our lives. That's what makes us so successful: we keep asking questions and seeking answers, and so we keep on learning.

That said, children are sometimes better at expressing this, and lots of the questions in the book come from kids. Did you ask lots of strange questions when you were young?

Zoe: Oh, definitely. Sometimes kids just view things in a completely different way. One of my questions when I was young was, 'Why have I got two daddies?' Because my dad was a public figure, so he'd be in the room with me, but he'd also be on the telly at the same time. And when I thought I'd figured it out, I was overheard bragging to my friend that 'my dad can get really small and go inside my telly'.

My dad's usually the person I go to with my most urgent questions. I remember ringing him up from an ancient amphitheatre on a cliff just to say, 'Dad, how the hell did they build this?'

QI Elves: Maybe we'll address that one in next year's book. The closest we get in this one is attempting to answer the question, 'If Rome wasn't built in a day, how long did it take (p. 211)?'

The British public gave us a huge range of subject matter to work with, from stardust (p. 43) to sandcastles (p. 182); from spies (p. 6) to Christmas crackers (p. 34); from chameleons (p. 102) to cheese sandwiches (p. 64) . . . It's a smorgasbord. And you've said before that every answer makes you think of another dozen questions, so we had a few for you, inspired by the content of the book.

Which two animals would you like to see a cross-breed of, in an ideal world (p. 207)?

Zoe: If you could cross-breed a zebra with a sheep and get stripy wool, that'd be quite fun. I love farm animals, and so I like the idea of combining them with something more exotic. Getting a giraffe's coat on a goat, for instance. Though I'm not sure how you'd physically cross-breed those two. Probably not going to be pleasant for anyone involved . . .

QI Elves: Are you scared of spiders (p. 178), or do you have other phobias?

Zoe: My daughter's terrified of spiders, so I spend a lot of time removing them from her sight, but I love them. And I believe if you flush them down the toilet or wash them down the sink, their friends will come and get you, so I always make sure to save them.

I'm generally not too bad for irrational fears, although whenever I get in the sea, I find myself singing the *Jaws* music to myself, which makes me quite nervous.

My son has trypophobia – the fear of small, closely packed holes. We bought him giant crumpets once, just to wind him up. He'll still eat them, but he has to smear them with something straight away to cover up the holes.

QI Elves: Would you go to the Moon if someone offered to take you (p. 46)?

Zoe: I used to always think, *No, I've got kids, what if something terrible happens?* But I've changed my mind recently. To walk on the Moon and be able to look back and see the world at a distance is too incredible an experience to turn down. And it would be great material for the show. If there's anything I can do that'll give me something to talk about on my programme, I'm up for it! So if Richard Branson's reading this, yes please, I'd like to go.

QI Elves: There are over 1,300 different pasta shapes (p. 18). Can you invent another?

Zoe: I'd like to see snowflake-shaped pasta, because not only are snowflakes very beautiful, but also each one is different, so you would never get bored of them. And also maybe teeth-shaped pasta, a bit like those teeth-shaped sweets you got as a kid. I want the grown-up version of that.

QI Elves: When was the last time you built a sandcastle (p. 182)?

Zoe: My brother and I always used to make boats on the beach, so I was quite good at those. Then one day one of my friends transformed our sandcastle-building by doing this incredible, Gaudi-style Sagrada Família sort of creation. The way you do it is you build some basic sandcastles right near the sea, then you get a bucket of sand that's wet and drip it through your hands, and it gives this sort of 'runny-down' effect. Once you've mastered that, you can make the most beautiful castle. We used to get really competitive and artistic.

QI Elves: We actually tried to do this trick on the latest series of *QI*, but none of the panellists' edifices were quite as impressive as yours, by the sound of it.

The apocalypse is coming. What one thing will you stockpile (p. 59)?

Zoe: Strawberry jam. Chocolate eclairs – the ones you chew. Bread and butter.

I don't need books. I've got so many piles of unread books. In fact, I wouldn't mind an apocalypse-type situation so that I could finally get around to reading them all.

Also can I have 1,300 types of pasta please? A packet of every shape.

QI Elves: In the book we write about the tradition of saluting magpies to avoid bad luck (p. 3). Do you stick to any superstitions like that?

Zoe: Not as much as some people. I have so many magpies in my garden it'd take over my entire life if I saluted them all.

My ex-husband Norm is very superstitious. When he was driving me to hospital while I was in labour with our son, he was so busy saluting a magpie that he very nearly crashed the car.

QI Elves: Well, let's see if your luck's held out with a game of Rock, Paper, Scissors.

Zoe: Always pick rock.

QI Elves: That's actually the opposite of what you should do (p. 122), but it seems to have worked in your case. Looks like the magpies are on your side.

What's your favourite question in the book?

Zoe: I'm a huge fan of 'Are zebras black with white stripes or white with black stripes (p. 71)?' A genius question, and I love the simplicity of the answer. And I'm slightly obsessed with zebras.

Another favourite: 'Why do we have two nostrils rather than one big one (p. 24)?' I have enormous nostrils; I've always thought I could house a large family up there. I used to win nostril-flaring contests at school.

QI Elves: Impressive.

Okay, since you can't call in to your own show, here's your one chance: what question would you like us to answer in the next book?

Zoe: I write down questions I want to ask you every week, and now that you've put me on the spot I've forgotten them all! All I can think of is: When we say, 'Heavens to Murgatroyd!' who is Murgatroyd?

A slightly niche question, perhaps, but now you've seen it I challenge you, dear readers, to get through this book without exclaiming, 'Heavens to Murgatroyd!' on every page.

For more from the team behind QI, visit qi.com.
You can also follow the Elves on TikTok, Instagram, Facebook and on QI's fact-filled Twitter account @qikipedia, and listen to their weekly podcast at nosuchthingasafish.com.

FUNNY YOU SHOULD ASK... AGAIN

Why do ladybirds have spots?

Ladybirds became distinctively patterned over millions of years of evolution in order to ward off predators such as birds and larger insects. There is a tendency in nature for brightly coloured things to taste revolting or even be poisonous, and it's in a ladybird's interest to warn hungry predators to stay away.

If a ravenous animal ignores these warnings, the ladybird can squeeze out toxic fluid from its leg joints to let the diner know that it has another trick up its knees. Despite this inventive yet disgusting protective technique, the collective noun for a gathering of ladybirds is a 'loveliness'.

There are around 5,000 different species of ladybird – almost equalling the number of mammal species – and while many of them are named after a certain number of spots, that doesn't actually help you to identify them. For example, the 10-spot ladybird can have anywhere between zero and 15 spots.

The UK is home to 47 different species of ladybird, but only 26 of them are easily recognisable as such, and of these, not all of them have the classic black spots on a red body. The pine ladybird is black with red spots, the orange ladybird is orange with white spots, and the striped ladybird is brown with both white stripes and white spots. In 2011, the 13-spot ladybird was rediscovered in the UK for the first time in nearly 60 years, so now it's slightly more spotted.

·············· THINGS WE SPOTTED ····················

❯ The Welsh for 'ladybird' is *buwch goch gota*, which translates as 'short red cow'.

2

Why do we salute magpies?

The rhyme 'One for sorrow, two for joy' has done a lot of damage to the magpie's reputation. There are different versions – including the more sombre 'One for sorrow, two for mirth, three for a funeral, four for a birth' – but they all tend to agree that seeing a solitary magpie is bad news.

Saluting the magpie and crossing yourself are superstitions that were developed by people desperate to counteract the bird's supposed bad luck. Some people prefer to recite a line like 'Hello, Mr Magpie, how's your wife today?' and in 1892's *All the Year Round*, Charles Dickens reported that in parts of Devon people would say the rhyme 'Clean birds by sevens, unclean by twos, the dove in the heavens, is the one I choose.'

There is an old Scottish legend that the reason magpies are unlucky is because they carry a drop of the devil's blood in their tongue. There was an additional belief that if a magpie scratched its tongue and then touched a drop of human blood, it would develop the power of speech. Other suggestions as to why they have such a bad reputation are that the birds didn't mourn Jesus's death correctly, or that they refused to go inside Noah's Ark and instead perched on the roof, while shouting and swearing loudly.

Magpies are scavengers, predators and omnivores – they eat berries, insects, eggs and baby birds – and even the RSPB has noted their 'almost arrogant attitude'. They are also extremely smart, with the same brain-to-body ratio as gorillas and chimpanzees – a figure outmatched only by humans. Perhaps we should really be saluting them out of respect rather than fear.

How does an ant measure distance?

If you want to know how far you've walked, there are several ways to find out: you could use a map, a GPS device or perhaps a pedometer to count your steps.

But what if you're an ant living in the Sahara Desert? Ants there never seem to get lost. They wander about over very similar-looking sandy ground, and once they find a piece of food they make a beeline straight back to their nest. There aren't really any landmarks to help them, and the shifting sands destroy any chemical trails left behind from their previous journey.

Ants are able to keep track of the Sun, so they know which direction they're facing, but to navigate their way home successfully they need to know how far they've travelled. Scientists hypothesised that if their stride length is constant, ants might be able to count their steps when moving around and then calculate the distance they've covered. A team from the universities of Ulm in Germany and Zurich in Switzerland conducted an experiment to see if ants really do count their steps, testing their hypothesis by fitting some of the insects with stilts.

The scientists set up a nest, and the ants were given a few practice runs without the stilts. They went out, collected food and walked back to their nest without trouble, but once they were given the stilts (made out of pig-hair bristles) they travelled too far, missed the nest and then began pacing up and down looking for it. Because the ants on stilts had longer legs and therefore took bigger strides, when they took their usual number of steps back to the nest, they overshot it.

After being picked up and manually returned to the nest, the ants on stilts were then able to go out and return home just as easily as they had in the past. This suggests they must have a way of counting steps – a sort of internal pedometer – to help them get around. Which is great news, because it's very hard to find a Fitbit that fits if you're an ant.

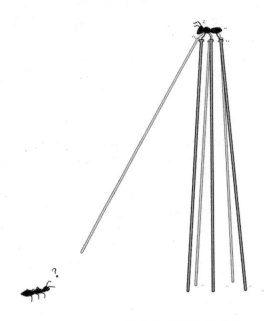

·····················F-ANT-ASTIC FACTS····················

❯ Ants can carry 50 times their own bodyweight.

❯ There are no ants in Antarctica.

❯ Male ants develop from unfertilised eggs, so they have a mother but no father.

Why are some spies called 'moles'?

Because of the novelist John le Carré.

This is the pen name of David Cornwell, who was working for the security services when he began writing. In French it literally means 'John the Square', and when asked about its origin, Cornwell claimed he'd seen it on a London shopfront and borrowed it.

As well as borrowing his name from shopfronts, le Carré borrowed words from the spy world, though he also made up his own jargon. The *Oxford English Dictionary* notes that espionage picked up the word 'mole' from le Carré's works, rather than the other way around. Le Carré said that the word may originally have been a KGB term for what the Americans would have called a 'sleeper' agent. He is also credited with creating the phrase 'honey trap'.

'Mole' isn't the only undercover word to have crossed over from the fictional world. Police nowadays refer to a 'sting operation', but the phrase was virtually unknown before the release of the 1973 movie *The Sting*.

Are there any other types of mole?

'Mole' can be used to mean someone who works in the dark. During the First World War, a team of sewer-diggers from Manchester became known as the 'First Moles' due to their phenomenal tunnel-digging speed: they could dig four times faster than their German counterparts.

Is there really such a thing as a '00' number and a licence to kill in the British Secret Service?

As far as we are aware, no.

Ian Fleming, the creator of James Bond, explained where he got the '00' prefix from in a 1964 interview with *Playboy*, saying, 'I pinched the idea from the fact that, in the Admiralty, at the beginning of the war, all top-secret signals had the double-0 prefix.'

Churchill's elite band of Second World War spies, the Special Operations Executive (SOE), did sometimes have code names that included a zero; the leading commando based in West Africa, for instance, was agent W01. Fleming was an officer in the Royal Navy's Naval Intelligence Department during the war and liaised with the SOE, so it's likely that this provided further inspiration, although he probably wouldn't have been able to reveal that information back in the 1960s.

As for having a licence to kill, as former MI6 agent Matthew Dunn has explained, there'd be little point. Whenever secret agents are working abroad, according to the laws of that country they're acting illegally – otherwise they wouldn't have to keep it a secret. If they get caught, no licence issued by the British government is going to pass muster with any foreign authority. Dunn did add that it was a shame, because 'It would have been great to whip out the Licence to Kill [as photo ID] when applying for membership to Blockbuster or the local library.'

Technically, James Bond isn't a secret agent at all. In MI5 and MI6, 'agent' refers to a civilian who volunteers as an informant or 'covert human intelligence source'. They're not formally employed by the Secret Service, but they agree to pass information on to them. Bond, as a professional spy on the MI6 payroll, would be called an intelligence officer.

. . . .

How did James Bond get his name?

Fleming took inspiration from a book called *Field Guide of Birds of the West Indies*, which was written by a man named James Bond. He later told *The New Yorker* that he wanted his main character to be 'an extremely dull, uninteresting man to whom things happened . . . When I was casting around for a name for my protagonist I thought by God, this is the dullest name I ever heard.'

How do organisations like the police name their operations?

....

In Britain, the police usually generate their operation names from a pre-approved list of words, including names of exotic birds or towns on the south coast. Officers aim to use words that are (a) unique, so there will be no confusion between operations, (b) cryptic, in case the name is leaked, and (c) appropriate – or, at least, not highly inappropriate. If an officer really wants to use a particular name, they usually can, so long as it hasn't been used before: Operations Crevice, Bagel and Poodle are among those that have been run by the UK police force. Themed names are also given to long-term initiatives; for example, Operation Blunt was set up to tackle knife crime.

Winston Churchill was very concerned about operation titles, at one point insisting that he approved each one beforehand. He even wrote a memo, advising that military operations shouldn't have overly confident or silly names. He didn't want soldiers' families to hear they had lost their loved ones in an operation called Bunnyhug or Ballyhoo. Instead, he recommended that they take their names from Greek or Roman mythology, constellations, stars, racehorses or war heroes.

The US military has a system called NICKA that provides naming guidelines and also archives all operations to avoid duplication. But names aren't chosen at random: high-profile campaigns are often given heroic-sounding titles, like Operation Inherent Resolve or Operation Just Cause, as a PR exercise. This new professionalism is probably an improvement on the previous system: Vietnam War ops included Operations Flip Flop, Hopscotch, Jingle Bells and Frequent Wind.

Why do American army personnel say,

ROGER DO YOU COPY ME ?

Why Roger?

To say that something had been 'received', you would send the letter 'R', and the military alphabet code for that letter was 'Roger'.

Today, the NATO alphabet (beginning 'Alfa, Bravo, Charlie') is used to give signals and avoid mishearing – e.g. confusing the letter 'M' with 'N' – but it isn't the first of its kind. The first phonetic alphabet to be used internationally was created by the International Telecommunication Union in the 1920s. It was based on the names of cities around the world and began 'Amsterdam, Baltimore, Casablanca'.

In 1941, the US military came up with the Able Baker alphabet. Its first entries ran 'Able, Baker, Charlie', and it had 'Roger' as its eighteenth entry. Two years later, the UK also adopted it.

However, Able Baker wasn't truly international, as it worked best for English speakers; some of the words included sounds that don't exist in other languages, such as Spanish. So the International Air Transit Association (IATA) devised a new version for the aviation industry, which began 'Alfa, Bravo, Coco'. This then formed the basis for the NATO phonetic alphabet, which came into force in 1956 and is the version we know and use today. It's very similar to the IATA version, but there were a few changes: 'Coco' became 'Charlie', 'Union' became 'Umbrella' and 'Extra' became 'X-ray', which is less confusing all round.

If a different alphabet had been in place at the time, then 'R' for 'received' could have been represented by 'Roma' or 'Romeo', but as it is, the Rogers have it.

. . . .

Reams of Rogers
Other, now largely obsolete meanings of the word 'roger' include a male goose, a ram and someone who catches thieves. It was also used as a familiar name for the devil ('Old Roger'), while in East Anglia a 'Sir Roger' was a small localised whirlwind.

Who was the original king of the castle and who was the dirty rascal?

This rhyme has existed in the form we know it for at least 200 years. But *2,000* years before you first sang it, your great-great-great-(add 80 more greats)-grandparents were doing almost the same thing.

In Roman times children would play a game, while singing and taunting each other, 'You'll be king if you do the right thing, and if you don't, you won't.' It's almost as catchy in the original Latin: '*Rex erit qui recte faciet, qui non faciet, non erit.*'

That's the Continental origin, but an alternative version surfaced on the other side of the Channel during the English Civil War. In 1651, a Scottish officer called John Cockburn was defending his fortress, Hume Castle, from Oliver Cromwell's English invaders. Refusing to surrender, he sent them the following letter:

> *I William of the Wastle,*
> *Am now in my castle;*
> *And awe the dogs in the town,*
> *Shan't gar me gang down.*

We don't know if Cockburn made this up himself or whether he was repeating well-known doggerel of the time. Either way, it didn't work: the castle walls were breached, and Cockburn and his men were forced to leave. But the rhyme outlasted his battlements, becoming popular and morphing into the one we know today. And so, in the British Isles at least, the English were the original dirty rascals to the Scottish king of the castle.

Why do we say someone is an 'unsavoury character' if they are unpleasant? If they were unsavoury, wouldn't they be sweet?

The word 'savoury' used to mean 'sweet'. It dates back to the 1200s, when it meant something or someone pleasant or agreeable. In the late 1300s, it evolved to mean a foodstuff which tasted good, then nearly 150 years later 'savoury' began to be used to describe bitter- or salty-tasting food, which has outlasted its earlier meanings.

The word 'unsavoury' originally meant 'flavourless', but evolved to mean something that tasted bad. Later, it came to be used to describe a person who was unpleasant.

Although 'savoury' has meant 'not sweet' for centuries, the proper term for the savoury flavour is 'umami', but it was not scientifically named until 1909. It was discovered by Japanese chemist Kikunae Ikeda, who analysed the chemical composition of seaweed broth and worked backwards until he isolated a chemical called glutamate, which is found in cheese, tomatoes, meat and other savoury foods. 'Umami' is a play on the Japanese word *umai*, which means 'delicious'. Ikeda's scientific paper wasn't translated into English until 2002, which may be why the idea is less well known in the Western world.

Puddings also used to be savoury (in the 'not sweet' sense). Originally, a 'pudding' was a 13th-century sausage made from the stuffed stomach, neck or entrails of a sheep or pig. We don't recommend serving it with custard.

Why are doughnuts called 'nuts' when they are made with flour?

Early doughnuts were called *olykoeks* (oily cakes) and were fried in pig fat. They were brought to America by Dutch settlers, who began arriving in the 1700s. The Dutch are also thought to have introduced pancakes, coleslaw and pretzels, and ship inventories show they brought their waffle irons across the seas too.

The doughnut hole didn't appear – or, rather, disappear – until the mid-1800s. If you believe his story, a sailor called Hanson Gregory created what he described as 'the first doughnut hole ever seen by mortal eyes' by using the top of a tin of pepper. The inside of the doughnut had tended to be stodgy, but the new ring-shape meant the snack could be cooked evenly throughout.

By the 1870s, you could buy special equipment for cutting out the holes, and doughnuts saw a huge surge in popularity in the 20th century, when they became a staple for American soldiers during the two world wars. Female volunteers, sometimes called 'Doughnut Dollies', would hand out the sugary snacks to servicemen stationed overseas.

But why are they called 'doughnuts'? Some people think it's because early recipes might have had nuts in the middle. However, our preferred theory is that, in the late 1700s, the word 'nut' meant a small rounded cake or cookie. This can be seen in both 'doughnuts' and 'ginger nuts', which are small spicy biscuits without a nut in sight. So the naming of the treats isn't quite as nutty as it sounds.

❯ The Tour de Donut is an annual bicycle race held in Illinois. Riders' times are reduced by five minutes for each doughnut they eat.

❯ The energy contained in a doughnut is about 450 kcal, similar to a stick of dynamite.

Why are so few nuts actually nuts?

Scientifically, the word 'nut' is defined as a dry fruit that contains a seed but doesn't split open when it reaches maturity. However, humans were eating nuts long before scientists came up with that definition; in fact, we probably started consuming them before we were even human. Today, most of us would simply define a nut as a small tasty snack that is delicious when salted or roasted.

NUTS

Hazelnut

Chestnut

DRUPES

Almond

Pecan

Walnut

LEGUMES

peanut

Of the things usually called 'nuts', hazelnuts and chestnuts fit the above definition, so technically speaking they are true nuts. However, cashews, almonds and pistachios are actually drupes – a fleshy fruit containing a single seed.

There is a similar muddle over the definition of a fruit. Technically, a fruit is the part of a plant that is fleshy and contains a seed, so despite usually being thought of as vegetables, pumpkins, cucumbers, tomatoes, avocados and okra are all actually fruits. However, rhubarb is in fact a vegetable.

Botanists must get very frustrated when shopping in a supermarket: broccoli is in the vegetable aisle but it is also a flower, and a banana is actually a herb, although it is stocked with the fruits. Peanuts are technically legumes (edible seeds which grow in pods that split open), which brings us back to nuts, which aren't actually 'nuts'. It's all quite a mixed bag.

····················· **PECAN YOU BELIEVE IT?** ····················

❯ A strawberry's 'seeds' are actually individual fruits themselves, containing even smaller seeds within.

❯ Brazil nuts are one of the few food allergens that are sexually transmissible.

How many types of pasta are there?

How long have you got?

Despite essentially being a combination of flour and water, the number of different shapes that pasta can take is virtually uncountable; for example, there are 26 varieties of alphabetti spaghetti alone. However, that hasn't stopped people from trying: according to food scholar Oretta Zanini De Vita's *Encyclopedia of Pasta*, the Italians are responsible for over 1,300 different shapes.

The difficulty comes in distinguishing between a distinct type of pasta and a different name for the same thing. *Cavatelli*, for instance, which means 'little hollows', look a bit like tiny hot-dog buns and have at least 28 different names, depending on where in Italy you're eating them. In Basilicata, in southern Italy, they are called *Orecchie di prete*, or 'priest's ears'. A similarly shaped but slightly longer pasta is known as *Strozzapreti*, or 'priest strangler', in Tuscany. These look like clerical collars, but the name is also linked to the idea that hungry priests would wolf the pasta down so quickly that they might choke.

Another holy-sounding pasta is *Su filindeu* – literally, 'threads of God' – which is eaten in a certain town in Sardinia. Just three women know the secret recipe, and they only make it for the Feast of San Francesco, which happens twice a year. It's a tradition stretching back 200 years. The mixture is kneaded extensively and there is a precise moment when it should be dried and cut: it needs to be just flexible enough to pull into long thin threads, but not worked so much that it will break. When Jamie Oliver travelled to Sardinia to learn how to make *Su filindeu*, he had to acknowledge defeat after it kept breaking.

If all that sounds kneadlessly difficult, then the world's newest kind of pasta could be the one for you. A team at the Massachusetts Institute of Technology has invented a shape-changing food that begins flat, then develops its structure when dropped into water. The hope is that it could be useful whenever food needs to be packaged as efficiently as possible, such as during space missions. Although it would be much harder to order any extra sides from zero gravity.

Why are all my loaves of bread either 400 or 800 grammes in weight?

The staple diet of Britons has long been bread and beer. Historically, this has meant that brewers and bakers have had to adhere to extremely strict rules. Even before 1066, if a brewer in Chester made bad ale, he would be forced to stand in a dung cart for a day, while in the time of Edward I, a London baker who sold adulterated bread could be dragged through the street with the offending loaf strapped around his neck.

In the 13th century, the laws were standardised as the Assize of Bread and Ale, rules that set out exactly what bakers and brewers could sell and what they could charge for their goods. The punishments for breaking these rules were strict, and it's where we get the phrase 'a baker's dozen', meaning 'thirteen': bakers would add an extra loaf to a batch of 12 to ensure that they didn't fall short of weight restrictions and end up on an unwelcome yeasty tour of the city.

Before England switched to the metric system in the 1970s, the standard weight of a loaf was either 14 or 28 ounces. Only buns and 'morning pastries' were exempt. 14 ounces is just under 397 g, so lawmakers decided to round up to 400 or 800 g. In 2008, the EU voted to remove this red tape, and it was decided that bakers could make bread any size they wished.

Jonathan Warburton, a fifth-generation baker from the Warburton's dynasty, hailed the new law, saying, 'This is a pretty historic moment,' and that the newly sized loaves would be 'fantastically popular with consumers'. But at the time of writing, a search of one popular online supermarket shows that the 13 most-purchased loaves are all still either 400 or 800 g in weight.

Why do we never get tinned broccoli?

You do, but only as soup. This is because broccoli doesn't survive the canning process intact.

For tinned food to be safe, it must be boiled to kill off any bacteria, sealed in the can and then heated again to make doubly sure. The process removes any oxygen, meaning mould and microbes can't grow in the tin.

Water boils at 100°C, but when cooked at temperatures of over 93°C broccoli quickly disintegrates into a mush. Even if the florets manage to keep their shape first time around, the second heating turns them into pulp. This has the added effect of removing many of broccoli's nutritional benefits. Worse still, the canning process ruins the flavour and colour of the vegetable, while at the same time intensifying its smell. Tinned broccoli would be a kind of off-green baby food that both smelled and tasted gross. If you didn't like broccoli to start with, you'd absolutely hate it in a tin.

Other vegetables that don't suit canning include cabbage, cauliflower, courgettes and (only Baldrick would care about this) turnips.

The best way to eat broccoli – and the best for you – is raw, including the stalk. Or try broccoli and Stilton soup – it's delicious, and you can hardly taste the broccoli at all.

Why does holding a spoon
get rid of the smell of garlic?

A clove of garlic contains two different substances, both of which are worth remembering the next time you play Scrabble. They are called alliin and alliinase, and are kept apart in separate cells in the plant, only mixing when the organism is damaged – for example, by being nibbled by an insect or crushed by a knife. The result of this blending is a smelly substance called allicin, which repels hungry bugs but tastes great in spaghetti bolognese.

Allicin contains sulphur, which has a pungent odour and is responsible for the smell of rotten eggs and drains. Sulphur can kill fungi, strengthen your car tyres, and is an ingredient in gunpowder, but it has another interesting property: it can bond to your cutlery.

It's easy to take cutlery for granted, since your choice of fork doesn't usually affect your dining experience, but that hasn't always been the case. Copper, bronze and silver spoons can leave a metallic taste in the mouth, and in the past not everybody could afford a cutlery set made from gold, which, because of its literal tastelessness, was popular with the upper classes. Napoleon III of France's cutlery was made of aluminium, which had no taste, but it didn't catch on because it quickly lost its shine.

Then, in 1913, a man from Sheffield called Harry Brearley tried adding different metals to steel, in an attempt to make a material strong enough to be used in gun barrels. Every time he created a dud, he would throw the offending piece into a corner. One day, he looked at the pile of rusting metal

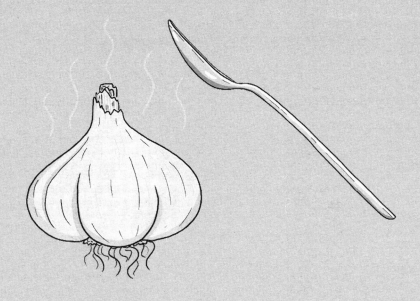

and realised that one piece hadn't discoloured. It was the first piece of 'stainless steel', and it revolutionised cutlery-making. Knives and forks that would stay shiny could now be made cheaply.

So what does this have to do with garlic? Well, Brearley's revolutionary steel is covered in a thin layer of chromium oxide, and the idea is that if you hold such a spoon in your garlicky hand, the metal forms a chemical bond with the sulphur in the allicin, removing the molecules from your skin. That's the theory, at least; nobody has ever done a scientific study to ascertain whether the technique works. It could be that if you stand there holding a spoon for long enough, your nose just gets used to the smell of garlic.

Why do we have two nostrils rather than one big one?

. . . .

Having two nostrils lets us detect a wider range of smells and do so more quickly than we would with just one larger one.

When analysing smells, our nostrils take it in turns to be the 'main' detector. You can check which one this currently is by holding one side of your nose closed, taking a breath and then switching sides – one nostril should feel slightly blocked. If you try the same trick a few hours later, the stuffed-up nostril may have switched. This is called the 'nasal cycle'.

There are odour-detecting sensory receptors high up in your nose. Some odours are absorbed quickly, and these are detected by the clearer 'main' nostril, while your other nostril detects the smells which need more time to bind to the receptors.

In 2006, a study at the University of California found that as well as being able to hear in stereo, humans can also smell in stereo. Theoretically, you can use your nostrils to work out where a smell is coming from, but to follow a scent trail you might have to move closer to it – for example, by getting onto your hands and knees, with your nose to the ground.

Moles have very poor eyesight and so rely on their sense of smell to find food and mates and to avoid predators. They have superior stereo smelling skills. Their two nostrils act independently, each one sending different signals to the brain, which then interprets those signals to determine the direction the smell is coming from. It's similar to the way that having two ears allows us to tell which direction a noise is coming from – our brains can work out how much time passes between a sound reaching one ear and then the other.

So, two nostrils are better than one, especially if you're a mole.

· NASAL APPRAISAL ·

❯ Humans can distinguish between more than one trillion different smells.

❯ You can't smell while you are asleep. You don't smell the coffee and wake up; you wake up and then you smell the coffee.

❯ If someone has anosmia, they can't smell anything.

❯ Dogs can tell identical twins apart. Their sense of smell is so good that they can smell the difference, even when the twins live in the same home and have the same diet.

❯ Male hooded seals attract mates by inflating the lining of one nostril and forcing air out of the other.

❯ The lamprey fish has only one nostril, which is found on the top of its head.

❯ Heliconia mites live in flowers and travel between plants in the nostrils of hummingbirds.

❯ There's a type of leech that lives exclusively up camels' noses.

❯ Following dental surgery, whenever Louis XIV tried to drink, liquid spouted from his nose.

Which of our lips is the most important?

Before we go picking favourites, we should point out that both of our lips are extremely useful. They help us to eat, speak, smile, frown and kiss. They're also unique in the natural world: humans are the only animals with lips that are turned permanently outwards.

Professor Gabrielle Todd has conducted experiments which have found that our bottom lip is a lot more sensitive than our top one and plays a bigger role in activities such as smiling and kissing.

So, like it or not, you really do have a stiff upper lip.

· *AMUSES-BOUCHES* ·

❯ Beavers have a second set of lips behind their teeth so that they can bite wood under water without letting water into their mouths.

❯ Actresses in black-and-white films wore green lipstick, which would show up better on old cameras.

❯ In the 16th century, a kiss was sometimes known as a 'lip lick'.

❯ Using too much red lipstick can make your urine turn the same colour.

Why do people get left and right mixed up, but no one seems to struggle with up and down?

. . . .

Which way is left and which is right is quite arbitrary. It can change depending on which way you're facing. Plus, you could be referring to your own left or somebody else's. On the other hand, it's easy to know which way is down.

Just drop something.

When you throw a boomerang, will it really come back?

It depends on which type you have. Boomerangs can either be 'returning' or 'non-returning', and the key is the shape of their edges.

The arms of a returning boomerang are shaped like an aeroplane's wings. This creates the shape needed for it to fly, the flat underside creating an area of higher pressure under the wing that keeps the boomerang airborne. Throw it hard enough, and at the correct angle, and it will fly in a rough circle through the air and come right back to you. And it won't take too long: a typical boomerang flight lasts just eight seconds.

A non-returning boomerang may sound like a fancy name for a stick, but they had many uses, particularly if you were a hunter-gatherer in the Australian outback. They were used in hunting (for clubbing prey) and for fighting, as well as for stoking fires, digging and clearing ground. Returning boomerangs could be used to imitate birds of prey, for scaring birds into a waiting net, and they were also used as entertainment.

The oldest surviving Australian boomerangs were found in a peat bog in South Australia and are about 10,000 years old, but the throwing sticks have an even older history outside Australia: archaeologists have found what seems to be a mammoth-tusk boomerang in Poland that is 23,000 years old. They were also used by ancient Egyptians – Tutankhamun even had his own set with gold tips – as well as Native Americans and rabbit-hunters in southern India.

Frisbees work in a similar way to boomerangs: the curved top of the disc creates a difference in pressure above and below the disc, making them soar through the sky. But while the original boomerangs were used to catch food, the first frisbees were used to carry it: they were made from pie dishes produced by the Frisbie Pie Company.

Why do the clocks go forwards in March and backwards in October?

. . . .

So we can enjoy the sunshine.

In 1784, Benjamin Franklin wrote a letter to the *Journal de Paris*, noting that the French could save money on candles in the evening if they just woke up a bit earlier. That way they could take advantage of the morning sunshine they normally slept through and enjoy lighter evenings. He recommended that 'Every morning, as soon as the sun rises, let all the bells in every church be set ringing; and if that is not sufficient, let cannon be fired in every street, to wake the sluggards effectually, and make them open their eyes to see their true interest.'

His suggestion wasn't a serious one – any money saved on candles would only end up being spent on the artillery alarm clock. But the idea behind his satirical letter is the same as the one that lies at the heart of daylight saving: if you get up an hour earlier in the summer, you get more sunlight in your day. Franklin was ahead of his time, and by a lot more than a single hour: it would be over a century before the idea was seriously considered.

In 1895, New Zealand scientist George Hudson lobbied his government to move the clocks forwards by two hours in the summer. Hudson did shift work and liked to collect insects in his leisure time. The more hours of sunshine there were in the day, the more time there would be for him to observe bugs. Unfortunately, the government didn't pick up on his idea.

The next champion of the cause was a British builder called William Willett, who happens to be the great-great-grandfather of Coldplay singer Chris Martin. He was annoyed that the Sun kept setting during his games of golf, so he suggested that the clocks should go forwards by 20 minutes a week for four weeks in the spring, and backwards again in the autumn. He published a pamphlet in 1907 called 'The Waste of Daylight', calculating that his measures would save the British public £2.5 million a year in lighting costs (over £300 million in today's money).

Willett died in 1915, just a year before his idea would become a reality. In 1916, because of the First World War, Germany introduced daylight saving time to preserve fuel, with the UK and her allies soon following suit. Its time had finally come.

· **EXTRA TIME** ·

❯ King Edward VII insisted that all the clocks at his country estate in Sandringham, Norfolk, should run 30 minutes fast, creating 'Sandringham Time'.

❯ On 6 November 2016, Emily Peterson gave birth to twins. Ronan was born at 1.10 a.m., and Samuel at 1.39 a.m. but Samuel was actually the elder since he was born before the clocks went back.

❯ In 1985, the American sweet industry put candy pumpkins on the seat of every US senator in the hope of extending US daylight saving time to cover Halloween.

❯ Venus rotates the opposite way to all the other planets in the Solar System, meaning for Venusians the Sun rises in the west.

Why is Christmas pudding sometimes called 'plum pudding', when it doesn't have any plums in it?

Originally called 'frumenty', plum pudding originated in the 14th century as a sort of porridge made of wheat boiled in milk with spices. It could be served plain, but some recipes included beef, mutton and even porpoise.

In the 17th century, it began to be thickened with eggs and breadcrumbs. Dried fruit and spices were also added, and it started to resemble a sweet pudding. In Yorkshire, it was eaten for breakfast on Christmas morning.

By the Victorian era, the recipe had settled on what we know as Christmas pudding today: dried fruit, sugar, breadcrumbs, eggs, spices, nuts and enormous amounts of alcohol.

So why call it 'plum pudding'? 'Plum' was an Elizabethan term that described all dried fruit, including sultanas, raisins and currants.

❯ Christmas pudding is traditionally made on 'stir-up Sunday' – the Sunday before Advent, five weeks before Christmas.

❯ Things added to a Christmas pudding over the years have included silver coins for luck, a wishbone for wealth, a thimble for thrift, a ring for marriage and a miniature anchor for safe harbour.

❯ Research shows that people who put their Christmas decorations up early are perceived as being more friendly.

Why do we pull crackers at Christmas time?

It all started in the 1840s, when a London confectioner and baker called Tom Smith took a trip to Paris. There he fell in love with the French bonbon – a sugared almond wrapped in twisted tissue paper.

Smith brought the idea back to the UK, and it was a hit. He started selling huge quantities, especially at Christmas time. They were mostly given as gifts to young, single women, so he began to include a small note inside the tissue wrapper, usually a love motto or a sentimental poem, which went down well with his Victorian clientele.

Although Smith patented his first cracking device in 1847, it wasn't perfected until 1861, when he named his new product Bangs of Expectation. You didn't unwrap these; you pulled them, creating a loud bang. The cracker business exploded, and by the 1890s, Smith was employing around 2,000 people. His crackers and paper hats were made by hand. Writers were commissioned to compose mottoes, and artists referenced popular crazes of the time, like jazz or the wireless, on the beautiful packaging. The Tom Smith brand continues to produce luxury crackers, and they supply the Royal Household, although the designs and contents are a closely guarded secret.

Over time, crackers became less romantic, and some included rhymes that were themed to appeal to particular groups, such as this verse penned for the Suffragettes in 1910:

We want (as quickly as we can)
To have our say
Most likely 'yes'!
And to become a match for man.

You might wonder why today's cracker jokes about 'Santa Paws' or 'mince spies' are always so terrible, and the reason is that they're supposed to be. The shared experience of groaning over a terrible joke brings people together. And isn't that what Christmas is all about?

····················· **EXPLOSIVE FACTS** ·····················

❯ Each Christmas cracker contains a tiny amount of gunpowder to create the bang.

❯ Every year approximately 1,000 people in the UK are injured by their Christmas tree.

❯ In Ukraine, Christmas trees are decorated with artificial spiders' webs.

❯ 'Farting Crackers' was early-19th-century slang for 'breeches'.

❯ A Yule Jade is a person who leaves work unfinished before the Christmas holidays.

Is it true that feeding your Christmas tree lemonade keeps it alive for longer?

. . . .

The evidence for this handy hint is flimsier than a festive fir after Twelfth Night.

Feeding fizzy drinks to Christmas trees is something that scientists, perhaps unsurprisingly, haven't spent much time looking into, so we contacted our friends at the British Christmas Tree Growers Association for more information. They told us there are 'no studies or evidence that giving a Christmas tree lemonade (or anything similar) will help. The best thing to do is make sure you keep it well watered (just plain water) and away from direct heat sources, if possible.'

. . . .

How should I dispose of a real Christmas tree?
An unusual option is to offer it to a zoo: some of them accept old trees, as their residents – particularly elephants, bears and meerkats – enjoy playing with them.

Should I just get an artificial one instead?
Possibly, but you have to use an artificial Christmas tree for 20 years before it becomes more environmentally friendly than a locally sourced real one. The oldest-known artificial tree still in use was originally bought in 1886.

What's so special about mistletoe?

In Europe, mistletoe has long had a reputation as a magical plant. Pliny the Elder, writing just after the time of Jesus, said that druids – the holy men who lived in France and Britain – considered it sacred. The word 'druid' is thought to come from an old Celtic word meaning 'the knower of trees', and they found mistletoe particularly unusual because it grows high up on tall trees and has no roots connecting it to the ground.

Today, we know the explanation for this is not so spiritual: mistletoe berries are eaten by birds, who then fly to the top of nearby trees and quickly poo out the seeds. Fertilised by the poo, a seed germinates and the plant lives a parasitic life, pulling water and minerals from its host tree until it's ready to create more berries, and the cycle starts all over again.

People in Europe (perhaps unaware of this bird-poo life cycle) began kissing under the mistletoe in the 1700s, but nobody knows why. The tradition was later popularised in America by Washington Irving, author of *The Legend of Sleepy Hollow*. In 1820's *The Sketch Book*, he described festive traditions he had observed abroad: 'The mistletoe is still hung up in farm-houses and kitchens at Christmas,' he wrote. 'And the young men have the privilege of kissing the girls under it, plucking each time a berry from the bush. When the berries are all plucked the privilege ceases.'

Mistletoe comes into its own just as other plants are withering and dying. Its berries shine brightly and there are no leaves on the trees to hide everyone's favourite seasonal parasite from view.

How many Christmas songs are there?

More than you can shake a yule log at.

A good place to start your tally is the Official Charts database, which records every song that has hit the UK Top 100 since 1952. Searching for 'Christmas' brings up 190 entries, including classics such as Wham!'s 'Last Christmas' and Wizzard's 'I Wish It Could Be Christmas Everyday'. It also turns up a raft of novelty singles, including 'Christmas in Smurfland' by the Smurfs and 'Have a Cheeky Christmas' by the Cheeky Girls. Twelve different versions of 'White Christmas' appear, including two by Bing Crosby (released in 1983 and 1985), as well as cover versions by singers ranging from Lady Gaga to Orville the Duck.

Expanding the search to include 'Santa' adds 41 to the tally, 'snowman' adds five, though curiously there are no titles featuring the word 'reindeer'. And that's before we've even considered classics like 'Silent Night', 'Away in a Manger' and 'Jingle Bells' – although 'Jingle Bells' was originally a Thanksgiving song, not a Christmas one, so its inclusion is debatable.

Trying to count traditional Christmas carols brings an additional festive layer of complexity. The English Folk Dance and Song Society's database contains 3,518 Christmas-related entries, and there are regional carols around the country to consider, with local specialities including 'The Sinner's Redemption' (Warwickshire), 'The Ten Joys of Mary' (Somerset) and 'King Herod and the Cock' (Worcestershire).

But this barely scratches the surface. If you expand the search to every country that celebrates Christmas, including the very first festive songs to the most recent, then the number is stratospherically huge. And it will continue to increase every time we reach the most wonderful time of the year.

. . . .

What about festive Christmas No. 1s?

You might expect that the songs which were at No. 1 on Christmas Day would be . . . well, Christmassy, but that tends not to be the case.

Since the UK charts started in 1952, and up to and including the 2020 chart, only five of the songs to hit the Christmas No. 1 spot have had the word 'Christmas' in the title: 1955's 'Christmas Alphabet' by Dickie Valentine, 1973's 'Merry Xmas Everybody' by Slade, 1974's 'Lonely This Christmas' by Mud, 1985's 'Merry Christmas Everyone' by Shakin' Stevens and 'Do They Know It's Christmas?' by Band Aid, which hit the festive top spot in 1984, 1989 and 2004. The last Christmas No. 1 to mention religion was 1990's 'Saviour's Day' by Cliff Richard.

Some Christmas songs chart in multiple years and eventually find success, albeit not on Christmas Day. Mariah Carey's 'All I Want for Christmas Is You' first reached No. 2 in 1994 but has charted every year since 2013, eventually reaching No. 1 in December 2020. 'Last Christmas' by Wham! finally reached No. 1 on New Year's Day 2021, 36 years after it was originally released, breaking the record for the longest time it has taken for a single to hit No. 1 after its initial release.

Why does the UK never win Eurovision?

If you think the UK has performed badly at recent Eurovisions because 'It's all political!', then you're not alone. But if you dig into the data, you'll find that this may not be the case.

The UK is one of the 'Big Five', alongside Germany, Italy, France and Spain, who provide a lot of the funding that makes the competition possible. In exchange, these countries are given a guaranteed place in the final, along with the host nation. This means they don't have to go through the semi-finals, where many of the weaker acts are told, 'Don't play that song again!' and are promptly sent home. The untested Big Five have to go up against performers who have all already proved themselves to be popular, and it often doesn't end well for them.

There's no denying that the UK has done terribly in recent years, coming in the bottom five on four occasions between 2017 and 2021. But if you look at the other countries in the Big Five during the same period, there are some similar stories: Germany has appeared in the bottom five every year except one, while Spain has really hit rock bottom, landing in the last five in each of those years. So if it's politics that is responsible for the UK underperforming, then that must be the case for Germany and Spain too.

France has done slightly better, but the only automatically qualifying country that has performed consistently well in recent years is Italy, which picks its participants with a popular and prestigious five-night TV spectacular called the Festival di Sanremo. Perhaps if we took a leaf out of the Italians' book and treated the competition more seriously, the glory days of Lulu, Bucks Fizz and Brotherhood of Man would come back. That sounds good to me!

· **EXTRA HITS** ·

❯ At the 1996 Eurovision Song Contest, due to a rule that said all featured instruments had to be on stage, Gina G performed alongside two computers.

❯ When ABBA won Eurovision in 1974, the UK awarded them zero points.

❯ Italy's performance at 1974's Eurovision was not

broadcast on Italian TV. The country's politicians were worried that the track 'Sì' ('Yes') would affect an upcoming referendum.

❯ The ABBA Museum in Stockholm has a piano that is linked to band member Benny Andersson's home. It plays whenever he sits down to practise.

What sort of song tends to win Eurovision?

. . . .

The last five songs to win the competition have been an Italian rock anthem, a Dutch piano ballad, a Portuguese jazz waltz, an Israeli electro-dance track sung partly in chicken and a Ukrainian song about the Second World War, with lyrics in the little-spoken Crimean Tatar language.

You might think that only the light, happy songs do well at Eurovision, but analysis by journalist Chris Lochery has shown that in the 21st century, twice as many songs in moody minor keys have won the competition. Another common misconception is that key changes are a sure-fire hit with the judges, but no song containing a change of key has come in first place since 2007. Tempo is also important: entering a song that is at or around 128 beats per minute is a disaster – seven of the songs that came last this century have been at or very close to this tempo.

But even if you have the best song in the show, the most important thing is to make sure that you don't perform second. No performer placed at number two in the running order has ever won the competition since it started in 1956.*

* The names of 10 UK Eurovision songs are hidden in the entries on pages 40–42. If you can find them, congratulations! (Turn to page 238 for the answers.)

Is it true that we are made entirely of stardust?

Not entirely, though large parts of us are.

Most elements in the periodic table began life in the stars. In a process called nuclear fusion, stars take lighter elements, like hydrogen and helium, and fuse them together to make heavier ones, like carbon and oxygen. When a star's life comes to an end, these elements are sent out into the universe, and in the explosive dying process some extra, heavier elements are also made.

The two most common elements in the human body are oxygen and carbon, which make up about 83% of our mass, and we now know that these are created in the stars. Other stellar elements found inside of us include nitrogen, calcium, phosphorus, sulphur, potassium, sodium, magnesium and a dozen or so more. So far, so starry.

However, there are three elements in the universe that are older than the stars. Hydrogen, helium and small amounts of lithium were originally created by the Big Bang over 13 billion years ago. About 10% of our mass is hydrogen, and we contain trace amounts of lithium too. That means some parts of us are as old as the universe itself.

How do we know what's at the centre of the Earth?

....

When there's an earthquake in Indonesia, you can feel it in India, and indeed in Indiana, but as you get further away from the epicentre, you feel less of the shake. Scientists can use these vibrations to work out what's inside the planet, because different materials wobble more than others. For example, if parts of the Earth were made out of jelly, they would shake much more than those made up of rock.

After measuring the quakes with their sophisticated instruments, scientists realised that under our feet there is a crust of earth, then a layer of rock called the mantle, which moves very slowly over time, and finally a core made of liquid metal. There had to be a liquid core because after an earthquake there is always a 'dark zone' on the exact opposite side of the Earth where no vibrations can be felt. It was reasoned that the liquid must cushion the effects of the quake.

But it turned out that wasn't the whole story. After a large earthquake in New Zealand in 1929, a Danish seismologist called Inge Lehmann noticed that tiny vibrations *could* actually be felt on the opposite side of the planet. Other scientists had noticed them but had explained them away as a problem with faulty seismographs. Thanks to her meticulous calculations, usually made on ripped-up cereal boxes, Lehmann realised that if the Earth's liquid centre was holding an even smaller solid core, then the discrepancy could be explained.

Lehmann's theory was finally confirmed in 1970, when the men and their machines caught up with her genius.

How do we know that greenhouse gases warm the Earth?

In 1824, a mathematician called Joseph Fourier worked out that the Earth should be a lot colder than it is, given the amount of heat that comes from the Sun. He calculated that we're kept warmer by our atmosphere acting like a blanket, which traps heat close to the ground. The eccentric Frenchman was obsessed with heat and would keep his rooms uncomfortably hot for visitors, while wearing a heavy coat himself.

Just over 30 years later, in 1856, an American scientist and inventor called Eunice Newton Foote collected an air pump, two glass cylinders and four thermometers and set about working out how this effect varied for different elements and molecules. She filled the tubes with gases, heated them up in the sunshine, and then timed how long it took for them to cool, eventually discovering that carbon dioxide was one of the very best gases at trapping heat. She wrote the first paper that suggested that the more greenhouse gases there were in the atmosphere, the more the planet would heat up.

By rights, Foote should be a household name, but she had three things working against her. She was an amateur, so her work was seen as less trustworthy. She was American, at a time when Europe was the centre of scientific discovery. And most importantly, she was a woman making groundbreaking discoveries in a man's world. So most of the credit went to an Irish physicist, John Tyndall, who came to the same conclusion three years later.

What would happen to the planet if someone blew up the Moon?

If it happened during daytime, surfers would be the first people to notice. The Earth's tides are mostly caused by the gravitational pull of the Moon, and while the Sun also has a small effect, the surf would be a lot less 'up' if the Moon disappeared.

That's bad news for surfers, but even worse for animals like crabs, mussels and starfish, which rely on the tides for survival. You might be able to go without a crab sandwich or some moules marinière, but many other animals rely on this seafood. The subsequent collapse of the tidal ecosystem would almost certainly lead to mass extinctions.

On land, much of the animal kingdom would also be in trouble, with many of them relying on the Moon for navigation or moonlight for hunting. Owls and lions would struggle to survive, but rats – who hide during a full Moon so predators can't see them – would likely proliferate.

The tides also drive ocean currents, which affect the planet's weather. Without any warm water moving around the planet, certain areas would grow hotter, while others would turn much colder. Extreme weather events would become more common than they are today.

Over the course of the next few millennia, things would get even worse. The Moon is a steadying influence on us, keeping our planet on a constant 23.5° tilt as it travels around the Sun. Without it, we would wobble. We'd lose our seasons and some parts of the world would have near-constant summer, while others would find themselves in centuries-long ice ages.

Finally, one bit of good news. The drag of the Moon on our oceans currently slows down the Earth's rotation by a tiny amount, so that a day gets around 2 milliseconds longer every century. A day lasted only 22 hours when the dinosaurs roamed the Earth. So, 4 million years after losing the Moon, we wouldn't need leap years any more, which can only be a boon for the calendar-makers of the future.

For the rest of us, though, the Moon disappearing would be terrible news. It's vital for our existence. So vital, in fact, that a large moon is one of the main things that astronomers look for when they're trying to find a planet that might be able to host complex life forms.

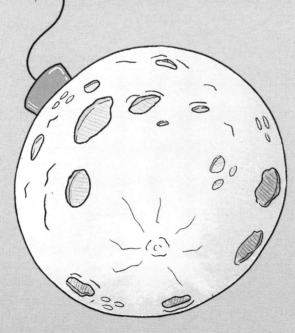

How big is a cloud? And how can you measure it?

The most accurate way to measure a cloud is to use a laser. If you place a device called a ceilometer on the ground, it can fire a spot of light all the way to the bottom of a cloud and determine how far from the Earth's surface it is. Calculating the height of the top of a cloud is trickier. This time your laser needs to be fired downwards from a satellite orbiting the planet. If you subtract the height at the bottom of the cloud

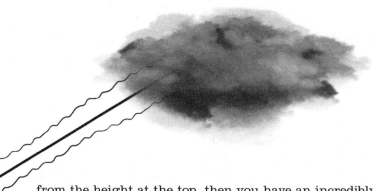

from the height at the top, then you have an incredibly exact measurement of its dimensions.

The size of a cloud can vary hugely, depending on what type it is and how much moisture it holds. If we take an average fluffy cumulus cloud drifting through the sky, it might measure a kilometre wide by a kilometre high. A cloud like that would contain about 500 tonnes of water – roughly the weight of 100 elephants. Despite this, it doesn't fall out of the sky because the weight is spread out over a wide area. Once the cloud gets heavier, it has to shed some weight, which falls as rain or snow.

But, of course, clouds can get much, much bigger. A 'supercell' is an enormous cloud that causes extremely violent thunderstorms. They're quite rare but can reach 18 kilometres in height and easily be 30 kilometres wide. A cloud like that would weigh some 6 billion kilogrammes, which is about the same as the Great Pyramid in Egypt. If you do see one, it's probably best to reschedule your trip to the beach.

Why doesn't the snow melt on mountaintops, where it's closest to the Sun?

You might be under pressure as you read this. Not just the pressure of needing to tend to various jobs, but also the pressure caused by all the air molecules pushing down on your head. If you were reading this at the top of a mountain, there would be fewer molecules directly above you and the air pressure would be lower. When the pressure drops, so does the air's temperature. It's the opposite effect to when you're pumping up a bicycle tyre: in that case you create more pressure, and so the valve gets warmer.

There's a secondary effect taking place as well. When the Sun shines on the Earth, the ground absorbs heat, which is slowly released back into the air over the subsequent days. The Earth's atmosphere acts like a duvet, keeping this warmth close to the ground. When you're at the top of a mountain, it's colder because you're further from this layer of warm air.

These two effects influence the temperature much more than the fact that the top of a mountain is closer to the Sun. The Sun is about 93 million miles away, while the top of Everest is only 5.5 miles up. So while you are, admittedly, closer to the Sun at the top of that mountain, it's the equivalent of somebody a mile away from you moving towards you by just the width of a blade of grass. That tiniest fraction of distance makes almost no difference to the temperature, which is why our snowy peaks remain.

Can you clean a pair of jeans by freezing them?

. . . .

We wouldn't recommend it.

The idea that freezing your jeans would kill off any germs and smells is a myth. Most of the bacteria on your jeans probably come from your body, and while you might think they would die at cool temperatures, they're remarkably resistant and you need only one to survive in order to cause a resurgence.

Despite the freezer idea being endorsed by Levi Strauss in the past, Levi's current CEO, Chip Bergh, has said it is an old wives' tale and doesn't work. Bergh has also admitted that he has a ten-year-old pair of jeans which he doesn't wash at all, explaining, 'I know that sounds totally disgusting . . . It's fine, I have yet to get a skin disease or anything else. It works.'

Whether you wish to try this experiment for yourself is entirely up to you, but we'll be sticking with laundry detergent.

How long would it take for a snowman to melt in the Sahara Desert?

As far as we know, nobody has carried out this experiment, so we're going to rely on some back-of-the-envelope maths to work out an answer.

It depends on a lot of things, like wind speed, the density of the snow or the height of the structure, but a 1.5-metre-tall snowman would melt in about eight hours in a greenhouse kept at 16°C, which is a good starting point for our calculations.

If we take 30°C as the average air temperature in the Sahara and imagine a snowman of around 70 kg and 90 cm tall (the height of an average seven-year-old boy), then it would be nothing but a puddle after about four to six hours. Although the Sahara has had some of the hottest temperatures ever recorded, so if your snowman gets unlucky, it could be sweltering under 55°C heat and probably wouldn't last 60 minutes.

In 1959, as a publicity stunt for a company that made glass wool insulation, a group of Norwegians transported a three-tonne block of ice from the Arctic to the equator in Gabon, crossing the whole of the Sahara in the process. It took them 27 days, and when they arrived at their destination, only 11% of the ice had melted. All they'd used to insulate the block was the company's glass wool.

The team also transported some important medicines, since they had space in the vehicle, and journalists were even given bits of the ice in a celebratory drink when the remainder of the block was flown back to Norway.

· **ICE TO KNOW** ·

❭ The tallest snowwoman ever made was 37.21 metres high. Her arms were two spruce trees and her eyelashes were made from eight pairs of skis.

Why don't women's clothes have pockets?

Blame the patriarchy.

Men's clothing has featured built-in pockets since the Renaissance, yet history shows that women had to wait a long time for them. And even when women did eventually get pockets, in around 1650, they were separate from their clothing and tied around wearers' waists. In fairness, the ones that survive today were generous by our standards – they could measure up to 30 cm wide and 40 cm long. Pockets were used for storing valuables, including the family's wages, and at night treasures were kept in them and tucked underneath a pillow. But they could also be utilised by thieves: one case seen by the Old Bailey in 1777 concerned a woman who had stolen two live ducks and hidden them in her pocket.

Towards the beginning of the 1800s, women's fashion became more figure-hugging, and unsightly duckling-sized pockets fell out of fashion. But most importantly, women weren't thought to need space to carry things, as anything important would be carried by their husbands. This practice, of course, suppressed women's freedom – if you couldn't carry money and other small items around, it was more difficult to live an independent life.

The end of the 1800s brought a little more equality, and as well as the vote women started to demand pockets. In 1895, a designer of women's bicycling costumes reported that many of her clients were requesting pockets so they could carry guns while riding. 'Not all of them want to carry a revolver,' she told

The New York Times, 'but a large percentage do and make no "bones" about saying so.'

The desire to have pockets also featured in a 1915 satirical suffragette piece titled 'Why We Oppose Pockets for Women'. Reasons given included: 'Because pockets are not a natural right'; 'Because the great majority of women do not want pockets. If they did they would have them'; and 'Because pockets have been used by men to carry tobacco, pipes, whiskey flasks, chewing gum and compromising letters. We see no reason to suppose that women would use them more wisely.'

A 2020 YouGov study found that 80% of women want pockets in their trousers, and that they have consistently asked for more of them. Are any clothing companies listening?

· · · · · · · · · · · · · · · · · · · **POCKET ROCKETS** ·

❯ Carrying a stolen potato in your pocket was an old English treatment for rheumatism.

❯ In the 1700s, wealthy Europeans would carry nutmeg graters in their pockets so they could season their food and drink.

❯ Zagreb has a Museum of Hangovers. Its inventor was inspired when a friend woke up one morning with an unexplained bike pedal in his pocket.

❯ The national dress of Bhutan has a huge pocket in the front known as a *hemchu*. People traditionally use it to carry their crockery around with them.

If you cloned yourself, would your clone have the same fingerprints as you?

No.

If your clone is genetically identical to you, all the instructions in your DNA for building 'you' – such as those that determine the colour of your hair and eyes – would match. However, some things, like fingerprints, are only partly determined by genetics. Your prints would more or less match those of your clone, but if you looked more closely, there would be slight differences.

Three months before you were born, your fingers grew a layer of skin, and then a second one underneath. The underlayer grew faster than the one on top, so it creased and bunched up because there wasn't space for it to lie flat. This created the individual ridges of your fingerprints. This process is quite random, and as a result so is the final pattern of your fingerprints. And there were other factors at play: the chemical balance around you as a foetus, and even the physical action of you squashing your fingers up against the wall of your mother's womb, resulted in subtle changes that made your fingerprints unique to you.

Can you identify someone's fingerprints from a photograph?

Yes. In 2021, police apprehended a criminal after he posted a photograph of a block of Stilton from Marks & Spencer. Unfortunately for him, his hand was also in the shot, holding the cheese, which meant his fingerprints were visible. The police were able to analyse them and identify him.

❯ The first person to be caught by fingerprinting was a student who was stealing medical-grade alcohol and drinking it out of a measuring jar.

❯ The only known fingerprint belonging to Michelangelo is on the bottom of one of his wax statues.

❯ There's an island in Croatia that is covered with drystone walls, making it look like a fingerprint from above. Locals have to keep chopping down trees to maintain its appearance.

❯ Until it was digitalised in 2014, the FBI's fingerprint database was kept on 83 million cards.

How do they put the stripes into striped toothpaste?

The easiest way to check is to open up your toothpaste tube. Some brands have multiple colours – red, white and blue, say – running through the entire tube like a French flag. Toothpaste is a non-Newtonian fluid, which means it can act like a solid or a liquid, depending on how much it is squeezed. When the various colours of toothpaste are first placed in the tube, they act like solids and don't mix together. But when you squeeze the tube, they act more like liquids and flow out onto your toothbrush.

Another technique used by toothpaste manufacturers is to separate out the white and the stripe. If you open up a tube of this type of toothpaste, you'll see regular white paste, with a small amount of paste the colour of the stripe – green, say – sitting at the cap end. Little extra holes close to the nozzle mean that when you squeeze, the white part comes out with green lines running through it, creating your stripes.

And it's not just different colours that can be put into a toothpaste tube. In 1961, Yuri Gagarin was the first person to eat in space. He was given toothpaste-like tubes filled with puréed meat, which he squeezed directly into his mouth. He then had a tube filled with chocolate sauce for pudding.

What's the strangest thing that anyone has ever stockpiled?

During the Cold War, the USSR kept a secret stockpile of steam trains on hand. This was in case their modern trains were taken out of service by nuclear bombs, or there was a shortage of electricity or a supply-chain issue with oil and diesel.

Switzerland has a stockpile of 15,000 tonnes of coffee beans. Swiss law requires coffee producers (plus producers of other goods deemed essential to life) to keep a stockpile in reserve in case of a national emergency. In 2019, the Swiss Federal Office of National Economic Supply suggested that as coffee isn't a life-or-death essential, it should be removed from the list of indispensables, but there was an outcry from the public, so it was allowed to remain.

Other unusual stockpiles include helium (in the US, originally for airships), cheese (also the US), pork (China), frozen fish (Malaysia) and plutonium (Japan). Many nuclear countries repurpose the waste products from their power plants to make nuclear weapons, but as Japan doesn't possess such weapons, its excess plutonium is piling up. The country currently has 44 tonnes going spare.

Was spam email named after the tinned meat?

Sort of.

Spam emails get their name from a Monty Python sketch in which two people are trying to order a meal in a café, but almost every option on the menu comes with spam, sometimes several portions of it. One customer protests that he doesn't like spam, so asks if it would be possible to have 'egg, bacon, spam and sausage' without the spam, but soon all conversation is drowned out by increasingly loud shouts of 'SPAM, SPAM, SPAM!' from everyone else in the room.

The word crossed over into general use, and then really took off when early Internet users described 'spamming' as what happens when people send multiple messages, drowning out the actual information with their 'spam'. Today, spam tends to take the form of those annoying emails which are mass-mailed to numerous accounts. Although, thanks to ever-more sophisticated filters, they should hopefully all end up in your designated spam folder.

Why does my stomach rumble?

The sound of your stomach rumbling is called borborygmi, and while it tends to happen when you haven't eaten for some time, it's not necessarily because you're hungry. The noise actually comes from your small intestine: when it's not had any food for a while, it starts its cleaning process, which makes the noise you hear as a stomach rumble.

How do you know when your food is 'piping hot'?
'Piping hot' refers to food that is so hot it makes a whistling or hissing sound. Just as some kettles whistle when they're boiling, if your food is noisy, it's ready.

.... CHURNING LEARNING ....
❯ In 1927, an owl was found that had another owl in its stomach, and that owl had a third in its own stomach.

Can you eat while hanging upside down?

You absolutely shouldn't try this because of the choking risk, but it is technically possible.

A healthy human body can digest food, regardless of whether you're lying down, sitting, standing, floating through space or, indeed, hanging upside down. That's because the forces your body applies to food as you're eating far outweigh gravity.

After you chew your food, you manoeuvre it to the back of the mouth with your tongue and push it into your oesophagus – the 20-cm-long tube that transports food to the stomach at speeds of up to one metre per second. Once in the oesophagus, the food is quickly passed along by rings of muscle running all the way down. These contract, narrowing the channel behind the food and squeezing it along, just like you'd squeeze toothpaste through a tube. There are also muscles running vertically from top to bottom that expand and contract, repeatedly making the oesophagus shorter and then longer again. This helps food move down, in the same way that a worm moves along the ground by expanding and contracting its body lengthways.

When food arrives at the stomach, it passes through an opening called the cardiac sphincter, which swiftly shuts behind it like a drawstring bag being pulled shut. After the food has left the stomach for the small intestine, another sphincter does the same to prevent the food going backwards. It's as though a series of drawbridges are being raised, or portcullis gates dropped, behind that mouthful of food, and there's no turning back. Gravity is powerless to stop the process, which is a good thing, otherwise astronauts couldn't eat in space.

The most common way this system backfires – literally – is if your sphincter muscles don't close the entrance to the stomach tightly enough. This causes gastric reflux, whereby stomach acid flows back up into the oesophagus. That's another reason why, unless you're in space and you really can't help it, it is best to remain upright while digesting food.

· · · · · · · · · · · · · · · · · · UPSIDE-DOWN TREATS · · · · · · · · · · · · · · · · · ·

❯ Some foodies advise flipping a burger in a bun upside down before you eat it. They argue that as the top of the bun is usually thicker than the base, it is better equipped to soak up any sauce and juices which may otherwise escape and leave you with a soggy bottom.

❯ In 2017, McVitie's declared that the chocolate on a chocolate digestive biscuit is technically on the bottom, not the top.

❯ If you turn a banana upside down and pinch the non-stem end, then it's easier to peel – and it also gives you a convenient handle for eating your snack.

Would a cheese sandwich rot in space?

Sandwiches rot thanks to the presence of oxygen, moisture, heat and bacteria, all of which are plentiful on Earth. Space, on the other hand, is essentially a freezing cold vacuum that contains no oxygen, water or, indeed, any other particles. And it certainly has no free-roaming bacteria looking for a meal.

If you eject a cheese sandwich from a spaceship, it will already be covered in its own bacteria (as everything is), but since there's no oxygen in space, and because any water will freeze almost immediately, the microorganisms cannot survive. So your sandwich will not rot, but it will still disintegrate. Eventually. The Sun emits radioactive cosmic rays and solar winds, which will bombard the butty and slowly break down the molecular bonds in the cheese, bread and, of course, your chosen selection of condiments (we recommend a nice chutney).

Inside a spacecraft it's a different story. Science-fiction fans may have the impression that spaceships are pristine, gleaming vessels inside and out, but this is not the case. You can't open a window, so they're more like the inside of a stuffy, sweaty submarine – ideal conditions for breeding bacteria that will feast on your sandwich.

Everything that usually falls to the ground on Earth – like beads of sweat, chunks of food and flakes of skin – floats in low-gravity environments, finding its way into every nook and cranny and getting sucked into vents and filters. In 1998, Russian cosmonauts aboard the *Mir* space station removed an inspection panel in the wall and discovered several football-sized globules of repulsive soggy gunk teeming with bacteria, mites and fungi that had been inadvertently collected by the air filtration system. In 2021, during routine swab tests, three brand-new types of bacteria were discovered in the International Space Station – one of them on the dining table. So, just like on Earth, astronauts have to constantly clean their living environment and keep a close eye on their food hygiene. Luckily, edible supplies are mostly freeze-dried and vacuum-packed to give them a minimum shelf life of nine months.

In fact, you're not very likely to see a cheese sandwich in space, because space agencies really don't like it when you spill crumbs in their spacecraft. In the 1960s, the US House of Representatives had to review an incident that took place during the Gemini 3 mission, when astronaut John Young revealed that he had smuggled a corned-beef sandwich inside his suit, all the way up into low Earth orbit. NASA was not amused.

.... ✧ ....

What actually _are_ nooks and crannies?
Nooks are the corners of a room, whereas crannies are small cracks and openings. If you've searched or cleaned every nook and cranny in a room, then you've done a thorough job.

Why, if we clean most things with hot water, do we brush our teeth with cold water?

It's all a matter of comfort. Hot water is better at loosening fats, which helps when washing clothes and dishes. To make a significant difference the water needs to be at a very high temperature, meaning your teeth would be cleaner but you'd scald your mouth.

A cold shower is almost as effective at cleaning you as a hot one (it's the soap and the scrubbing that makes the difference), but we warm the water because it feels nicer.

···················NOTHING BUT THE TOOTH···················

❯ You can sprain your teeth.

❯ Your dentist can smell whether you're scared of them.

❯ As well as a cure for bad breath, Listerine has been marketed as an antiseptic, a floor cleaner, a treatment for gonorrhoea, toothpaste, deodorant and a cure for dandruff.

66

How do you wash a raspberry?

It's more a gentle dip than a hearty scrub.

For the hygiene-conscious, all those little bumples are a nightmare – is there a Swiss Army knife with a raspberry-crevice cleaning tool? Then there are all those minuscule hairs to deal with. Should you google 'raspberry hairbrush'? Can you get raspberry shampoo?

You don't need to worry about any of that. It turns out you shouldn't really 'wash' raspberries at all. If you run them under the tap, you'll bruise them and make them all mushy, so you're meant to just put them in a colander, lower it into a bowl of cold water and gently swish it around. Then, you allow the moisture to drain away, or if you prefer, you can line a salad spinner with paper towels and gently spin the berries in that. No need to dry each hair with a teeny-weeny raspberry hairdryer.

The bumps on a raspberry, by the way, are called 'drupelets', and each one of them is a tiny individual fruit. A raspberry is a fruit colony – a so-called 'aggregate fruit' – rather than a single fruit. The miniature hairs are called 'styles' (has anyone told Harry?). There are more than 50 drupelets on a raspberry. The exact number is directly related to the number of times a bee has landed on the flower to pollinate it. No need to worry about that either: bees make sure to keep their feet clean; they even wash their eyes.

The word 'drupelet' comes from *druppa*, ancient Greek for 'wrinkled', while 'styles' is from the Latin *stilus*, a 'pin' or 'stalk'. But nobody knows where 'punnet' comes from.

Or, indeed, the word 'raspberry'.

Why do we say 'sweating like a pig' if pigs don't sweat?

We often talk about pigs rather unfairly. We say 'living in a pigsty' despite pigs being fairly clean animals – though they do like rolling in mud to cool down. Crucially, they do so because they can't sweat, which makes the 'sweating like a pig' idiom somewhat baffling.

The phrase has nothing to do with the pigs you might see out in a field and everything to do with the process of iron smelting. Hot iron is poured onto sand, where it cools and becomes solid, creating a crude kind of metal known as 'pig iron'. The name is said to have come from the layout of the moulds, which creates bigger pieces alongside smaller ones, so the shapes are similar to seeing a sow with her piglets. Drops of moisture form on the pig iron as it cools, and when the metal is 'sweating like a pig', that means it has cooled and is ready to be handled.

.... SCRATCHINGS ....

❯ Pigs can be taught to play video games.

❯ There are more pigs in Spain than humans.

❯ Feral hogs in Canada build their own houses. They are known as pigloos.

Why are cats' tongues so much rougher than dogs' tongues?

If you look closely at a cat's tongue, you will see that it is covered in hundreds of tiny flexible curved spines called papillae. These turn cats' tongues into incredibly effective combs. Not only do they remove loose fur, fleas and dirt, but they also spread saliva evenly throughout the fur, helping cats to stay cool.

In bigger cats, such as tigers, tongue spines have another function, helping these predatory animals strip fur and meat from their prey when they eat them. A housecat's lick just feels a little rough, like sandpaper; a tiger's, on the other hand, is rough enough to draw blood.

Cats are solitary hunters, so they need to be well groomed in order to hide their scent from their prey and dangers such as larger cats. Dogs hunt in packs and rely on each other to chase down prey and avoid danger, so they don't need the same level of grooming. This means they have softer tongues than cats, which is good news if you have an especially licky canine companion.

······················· FUR REAL? ·······················

❯ Dogs can have cat allergies – and vice versa.

❯ The first-ever English novel is about talking cats.

❯ Cats farm bacteria in their bottoms.

❯ Dogs can suffer from a strained tail if they get too happy.

Don't zebras' stripes make them stand out like a sore thumb?

Not to lions.

No one really knows why zebras evolved stripes and what exactly they're for. One theory is that a zebra's coat acts as simple pattern camouflage, allowing it to blend in with the background like a soldier in combat uniform. It doesn't matter that their stripes are black and white and the tall grass around them is yellow, brown or green because their main predators, lions, are colour-blind.

A zebra standing still in grassland may be pretty much invisible to a lion, but zebras don't stand around on their own that much. They tend to travel in large herds, keeping close together, and some believe this is where the stripes really come into their own. From a lion's point of view, the pattern of each zebra's stripes blends into that of all the other zebras around it, befuddling the lion so that it sees only a huge mass of wavy lines, unable to make out where one zebra ends and the next one begins, and even finding it hard to tell which way the herd is moving. Because they can't make out any individual animal, the lions can't identify the younger or weaker zebras who would be easier targets. (Appropriately enough, a group of zebras is called a 'dazzle'.)

Zebras, incidentally, are among the few mammals that *aren't* colour-blind, and their night vision is about as good as an owl's. Lions also have excellent night vision, but despite this – and the fact that they can run faster than zebras – they catch only 25% of those they chase.

The zebra's stripes have another function: they make

it easier for zebras to identify one another. Like human fingerprints, every zebra's coat has a slightly different arrangement. This enables a mother to quickly pick out her foal in a crowd, and allows any zebra to tell at once whether a herd is theirs or not.

New research suggests that zebras' stripes may also help to regulate their temperature. Those in hotter areas tend to have more stripes, and the theory is that the air moves at different speeds over the black and the white areas, creating a swirling current that keeps them cool.

And finally, the zebra's amazing coat might also be useful in deterring disease-ridden biting insects. Like lions, the insects are confused by the pattern, causing them to abort touchdown or else fail to decelerate and crash-land. The scientists behind this theory have proposed that ordinary domestic horses could be protected from flies by dressing them in zebra-skin coats.

· ·

Are zebras black with white stripes or white with black stripes?

Zebras are black with black and white stripes.

If you shave a zebra, you will see that their skin is black, suggesting that this is their primary colour and the black and white stripes grow on top.

What's the difference between antlers and horns?

all bone

keratin
Bone

Horns and antlers have the same purpose: to protect against predators, and (for males) to fight other males and attract females.

Antlers belong to animals in the deer family (technically known as the Cervidae). Made entirely of bone, they are extensions of the animal's skull, and they tend to fall off each year, growing back in time for the next breeding season.

Horns are found on the Bovidae family, which includes sheep, goats, cattle, antelopes, bison and buffaloes. Unlike antlers, they aren't 100% bone; they have a little core of bone, but the majority is an exterior 'sheath' made of keratin. Once fully grown, the horn is usually there for life, although there are a few exceptions, such as the North American pronghorn, which regrows its horn every year.

A rhino is often said to have a horn on the end of its nose, but it's not a horn at all. It's made entirely of keratin and lacks the bony core that normal horns have.

....

Why do the horns of baby deer look softer?

Until they are fully grown, a deer's antlers are covered in 'velvet' – a layer of skin that contains blood vessels, which supply them with oxygen as they grow. This is why the antlers of young deer look lovely and soft: they actually *are* soft while they're still growing. After the velvet comes off, the hardened bone beneath is revealed.

During growing season, deer can grow nearly an inch of antler every single day. They even siphon off nutrients from the rest of their skeleton, essentially robbing their other bones to build their antlers.

··············· **POINTERS** ·····························

❯ The extinct Irish elk, or *Megaloceros giganteus*, had antlers that could span over 3.5 metres – the widest ever recorded.

❯ Moose use their antlers as hearing aids that funnel sound towards their ears.

Can goldfish hear?

Not only can goldfish hear, their hearing is better than that of most other fish.

Goldfish don't have external ears, but otherwise their hearing apparatus works in the same way as ours: sound waves collide with their eardrums and cause vibrations through tiny bones called ossicles and otoliths. These feed up to the brain, which then interprets the signals as noise (for more on human hearing, see p. 133). What makes goldfish special is that they also use their swim bladders as sound boosters.

Swim bladders are gas-filled sacs that some fish use for buoyancy, inflating and deflating them to move up and down in the water. But a goldfish's also wobbles around when sound waves hit it, and bones connecting the swim bladder to the inner ear convert this wobbling into sound. The swim bladder can pick up a far wider range of noise than the otoliths alone, meaning a goldfish can hear sounds that are ten times more high-pitched than, for instance, a cod could. It's the equivalent of us humans using our lungs to help us hear better.

The quietest sound that a human can hear measures 0 decibels. It's not quite silence, but it's not far off. However, fish hearing only starts at 60 dB. That's about as loud as a normal human conversation, so if you ever want to keep a secret from a fish, just stick to a whisper.

Can dogs tell the time?

Dogs certainly seem to recognise certain patterns, such as when their owner will be home from work or when their next meal is due. Like most mammals, they have a circadian rhythm, which is a 24-hour cycle that regulates sleeping and eating times.

Dogs may also mark time by using their sense of smell. If a dog's owner usually comes home at the same time every day, then the person's scent levels around the house will be at their lowest point just before they return. The dog may use this, rather than any sense of time passed, to work out that this low level of odour usually means the imminent return of both their owner and their familiar scent. BBC Two's *Inside the Animal Mind* ran an experiment in which several sweaty shirts belonging to a dog's owner were placed around his house shortly before he was supposed to come home. As a result, the dog didn't get up to wait for him like it usually did, because it hadn't registered the expected drop in scent levels.

Why is it so hard to win a prize at a funfair?

. . . .

The games at a funfair are designed to look simple, but they leave success tantalisingly out of reach for most players, which keeps us coming back for more.

Take the simple basketball throw: one trick to make it harder is to have the basket higher than regulation; others include having an oval hoop instead of a round one, putting decorations around the ring to interfere with your depth perception, and overinflating the ball so that it bounces away from the target after even the slightest touch of the rim. A popular YouTube clip shows a college basketball player at a funfair trying what for him should be a routine shot, but he misses the first five times, before eventually scoring his basket. This partly explains the success of fairground games: they can't be impossible or people would never play; there have to be just enough winners walking around with an oversized cuddly toy to make you think you have a chance of winning too.

There's a trick for every game: the milk-bottle pyramid might have lead weights in its base; trying to burst a balloon with a dart can feature underinflated balloons and blunt darts; and the hoops on the ring toss are made of especially hard plastic, which means they are a lot more likely to bounce around than settle gently over your target.

There are some ways to tilt the odds slightly in your favour. The 'wobbly ladder' is simply a game of skill that can be mastered. The trick is to ignore the rungs and climb up the two ropes, moving right arm and left leg at the same time, then vice versa. The classic 'test of strength', meanwhile, is actually a test of accuracy. Concentrate more on hitting the centre of the target with a downwards force rather than striking it as hard as you can.

Okay, so things aren't exactly how they seem in a fairground, but is that really unreasonable? The owners need to make money, which means they can't give away more in prizes than they take in payment. What you're paying for is the experience of trying your luck against the game-maker's knowledge. Sure, you could bypass the funfair completely, go to a toy shop and simply buy a teddy bear that's twice the size of the child who will own it. It might be more fair, but where's the fun in that?

Has there ever been a strike in a bowling alley?

. . . .

Rarely, if the QI Elves are on a works outing. However, if you're talking about the other kind of strike – people downing their tools and stopping work – then that was surprisingly common in the early days of 10-pin bowling.

Pre-mechanisation, bowling alleys employed adolescent workers called 'pin-boys'. They would sit on a ledge at the end of the bowling lane and jump down between turns to reset the pins and return the balls. If you tipped them well, they would set the pins up slightly closer together to make them easier to knock down. If they took against you, they could negatively affect your game. In 1913, a writer in the *Baltimore Sun* said that 'The pin boy has no conscience. He will set up pins with all the haste of a snail and then, straddling his railing, swing his foot in front of just where you want to bring in your best left-handed curve, heedless of personal jeopardy. He will spoil shot after shot and pick up the pins, whistling merrily, unless for a moment he happens to be busy arguing with the boy in the next alley.'

The boys were badly paid, and it was dangerous work that often involved dodging balls thrown by the wealthy patrons. And so, in 1932, when one alley owner in Saskatchewan forced his boys to either clear snow or be fired, there was a walkout. This was the catalyst for a spate of strikes over the next decade, especially in Canada, as the boys insisted on better conditions and fairer pay.

No worker – especially one who works in a bowling alley – deserves to be in the gutter.

What's the oldest sporting competition in the world?

In 1360, a group of Ottoman soldiers organised an oil-wrestling competition, which they called Kırkpınar. Well over 600 years later, the 659th annual Kırkpınar was slated to take place in 2020, but tragically had to be cancelled due to the global coronavirus pandemic.

Kırkpınar is quite a spectacle. Around a thousand men, wearing leather shorts and covered in olive oil, pair off and grapple until a competitor is either pinned to the ground or lifted above the other's shoulders and carried for three steps. If there's no winner within 40 minutes, there's 15 minutes of extra time, during which points are given for technique. However, this is a recent innovation; before that, individual bouts could last for days.

The competition continues for around a week, until a single wrestler is left standing. In total, about two tonnes of olive oil are used during the event, enough to make dressing for over 77,000 salads.

······················ SPORTS THOUGHTS ·····················

❯ Yamaha has invented an app that allows sports fans to cheer their teams remotely, with the recordings played straight into the stadium.

❯ Early racewalking allowed you to run for part of the race if you needed to ward off cramp.

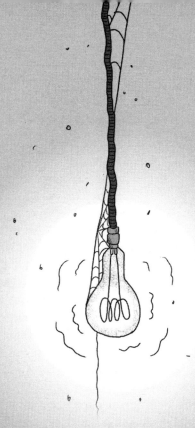

What's the longest anyone's left a light on?

120 years.

There's a bulb at a fire station in California that has been illuminated since 1901. It took a brief break when it was moved between two different stations, but the bulb, more formally known as the Livermore Centennial Light Bulb, holds the Guinness World Record for the longest-burning light bulb.

Does electricity consumption peak at certain times of day?

Yes, and it's because of our combined love of tea and television.

The increased demand for electricity around big televised events is known as 'TV pickup'. It usually happens when viewers go to make a cuppa or open the fridge to grab a snack during the ad break or at the end of a popular programme. Electric kettles use quite a lot of energy for their size, and when lots of them are turned on at once, it puts a strain on the electric grid.

To keep everything flowing as it should, the National Grid has a dedicated team tasked with forecasting these surges and working out how to supply the electricity required. They keep an eye on soap operas, to time pickups with the exact moment the closing credits roll, and they even follow popular plot lines to plan for dramatic moments that might attract high viewing figures. Sport plays a big part too: when England lost to Germany in the 1990 World Cup semi-final, they saw a pickup of 2,800 megawatts – that's the equivalent of around 1.4 million Britons making commiserative cups of tea.

With a huge number of channels now available and streaming services making programmes available on demand, these spikes have reduced significantly. Surges do still happen, though, around events such as royal weddings, World Cups or the Christmas Day TV schedule. The energy required is drawn from a number of sources, all ready to supply extra electricity at a moment's notice. The Dinorwig Power Station in Wales uses hydropower to help out, releasing vast amounts of water from its reservoirs into massive electricity-producing turbines. These can generate 1,728 megawatts of energy in just 16 seconds, ensuring that we can all pop the kettle on at once. Who knew a cup of tea was quite so powerful?

· · · · · · · · · · · · · · · · · ·PEAK YOUR INTEREST· · · · · · · · · · · · · · · · · · ·

❯ The two-hour-long final episode of *M*A*S*H* was watched by about 125 million Americans. When it finished, the 1 million New Yorkers flushing their toilets released an extra 6.7 million gallons of water into the city's sewers.

Will we ever be able to catch a bolt of lightning and capture all that free energy?

A single lightning bolt can contain up to 10 billion watts of energy, which means just a couple of bolts could theoretically power all the microwaves in the UK. There are a few practical problems with this idea, though, the first being that we don't have many devices that can deal with such an enormous surge of energy. We also don't know where lightning will strike, and when it does, it only does so for two-hundredths of a second – not nearly long enough to cook a lasagne.

That's not to say that people haven't tried to harness the power of the heavens. In 2007, a company in Illinois claimed to have powered a 60-watt light bulb for 20 seconds using the power from a lightning bolt. They had hoped to be able to store the electricity for future use, but told the press, 'Quite frankly, we couldn't make it work.' In the 1960s, the CIA hoped to use lightning for more nefarious means: to assassinate enemies and make it look like an act of God. They shelved the idea since it would only have worked if their target was outside in the middle of a thunderstorm, and they would have needed to dangle a huge, conspicuous wire from an aeroplane in order to direct the bolt to its target.

So lightning is destined to remain far less practical than other weather phenomena, such as the sun and the wind.

How do you pronounce 'Shrewsbury'?

It's 'Shroosbury' . . . usually.

For centuries, the name has been pronounced in a number of different ways. Some people say 'Shroosbury' (to rhyme with 'blues-bury'), others 'Shrowsbury' (to rhyme with 'throws-bury'). In 2015, the town hosted a debate between historians, and the *Shropshire Star* ran an online survey. Of over a thousand participants, 81% voted that 'Shroosbury' was correct.

When the *Shropshire Star* asked around, they found that the town's mayor was disappointed, saying, 'It is absolutely "Shrowsbury" . . . due to the Old English spelling of the town's name.' He was contradicted by the town crier, who always pronounces it 'Shroosbury', although he claimed not to be that bothered as there had been 'about nine different ways to pronounce the town's name' since medieval times. The local MP and town council leader both called it 'Shrowsbury', the town clerk preferred 'Shroosbury', and most residents the paper spoke to preferred 'Shroos' too. As one resident said, 'Did Shakespeare write the *Taming of the Shrow*? I think not!'

In fact, the name has nothing to do with a shrew. Shrewsbury was originally recorded as 'Scrobbesbyrig' by Anglo–French scribes in 1016, a word that may have meant something like 'the fortified part of the shrub or scrub'. The name mutated over the centuries, partly thanks to the scribes who found the 'scr' hard to pronounce and wrote it as 'Sciropesberie' instead. The newer spellings 'Shrouesbury' and 'Shrewesbury' have both been around since the 1300s, so while 'Shrews' seems to have won the spelling war for the moment, there are probably a few more centuries of argument ahead.

Who decided what letters went where on a keyboard, and why aren't they in alphabetical order?

The 'who' is easy to trace: 19th-century newspaperman and inventor Christopher Latham Sholes came up with the QWERTY keyboard layout in 1872. The 'why' is more difficult.

Four years earlier, Sholes, along with printer Samuel Soule and inventor Carlos Glidden, patented a new form of typewriter in order that the user 'may print his thoughts twice as fast as he can write them'. The keys were laid out like a piano keyboard and put in alphabetical order, so early typewriters were also known as 'literary pianos'. Four years later, the keyboard configuration we recognise today was invented by the same team.

There's no record of why Sholes chose that arrangement, but there is plenty of speculation. Some commonly paired letters – for example, 's' and 'h', 'c' and 'k' – were distanced from each other, and many claim this was to slow typists down, because when they typed too fast, the keys jammed. But speed wasn't an issue because touch-typing wasn't developed until 1888, so this seems unlikely. Nor is it true that the most common letter pairings were placed far apart: 'e' and 'r' is the second most common pairing in English, and those keys are side by side, while 't' and 'h' is the most common, and they're diagonal neighbours.

Another theory is that the keyboard was developed to suit telegraph operators transcribing Morse code. The symbols for 'z' and 'se', for instance, are often confused in Morse, and on a QWERTY keyboard those keys are close to each other so that the typist can quickly delete a 'z' and replace it with an 'se', if needed.

Finally, it's often suggested that the design allowed typewriter salespeople to impress customers by writing out 'typewriter quote' using only letters that are found on the top row. It's a neat theory, but there's no documented evidence for it, and it's unclear why that would be key to a sale.

The likely truth is that Sholes employed both logic – for instance, trying to make life easier for telegraph operators and secretaries – and randomness in his design. And the reason we still have it today is that we're very susceptible to what psychologists call 'status quo bias': once something is established, even if it doesn't work perfectly, we're extremely reluctant to change it. For example, when was the last time you changed your utility provider?

Why is a computer mouse called a 'mouse'?

The first computer mouse was designed in the 1960s by staff at the Stanford Research Institute in America. It was wooden, with one button on the top, two wheels so that it could be pushed forwards and backwards or side to side, and a wire sticking out of the back. When asked why it was called a 'mouse', Doug Engelbart, who had had the original idea, said, 'It just looked like a mouse with a tail, and we all called it that.'

We can be thankful they came up with a snappy nickname, as the device was originally called the 'X–Y Position Indicator for a Display System'.

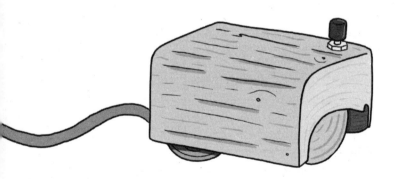

How is Bubble Wrap made?

. . . .

Bubble Wrap is a trademarked name, owned by the American company Sealed Air. Other 'cushioning laminates' are available, but this is how Sealed Air does it.

The process starts with gravel-like resin pellets. These pellets are sucked into a barrel called an extruder, which melts them down at temperatures of over 450°C. The plastic goop then cools and is turned into a film, which is squeezed out of the machine in the form of two layers of clear plastic. These are pushed through a series of rollers to ensure they're the right thickness.

To get the bubbles in, the top layer of the film is then wound around a special cylinder with lots of holes that looks a bit like a honeycomb. A powerful vacuum is applied from inside the cylinder to suck the plastic inwards, so it takes on the exact outline of the holes, creating the topmost 'bubble' shape. After the top layer is finished, the second layer of film is stuck onto the first one to make the base, trapping the air inside. The wrap is then cut down to size, perforated and transported in huge rolls.

Bubble Wrap was created in 1957, when its inventors were trying to make a textured novelty wallpaper. They stuck two shower curtains together and ended up with a sheet of bubbly plastic. It didn't take off initially, but in the 1960s they hit on the idea of selling it to IBM, which had recently launched a new computer and needed a way of protecting it in transit. This was much more effective than the previous best method of insulating fragile packages – using balled-up newspaper – and the product's sales 'bubbled up' from there.

How do manufacturers produce hundreds of ripped jeans that all look so similar?

. . . .

That 'naturally worn-out' look requires artificial and very precise processing. First, manufacturers have to decide on the type of tear they want. As any denim connoisseur will tell you, there are three main types of rips:

(1) *Scrapes*: small surface wounds, which don't penetrate all the way through the material.
(2) *Shreds*: tears where the hole is partially covered by threads running across it.
(3) *Holes*: holes.

The simplest way to distress jeans is to rub away at them by hand, using sandpaper or pumice stones, but for speed and consistency, companies instead deploy 'denim destroy machines', which can achieve the desired effect in just seconds. A design is programmed into a computer that's attached to a laser gun, and this burns the desired shapes into the garment. Smaller scuffs require the jeans to smoke for a short period, while for bigger tears they are briefly set on fire. It takes just 90 seconds for a laser to completely distress a pair of jeans, while it would take about 10 minutes to do it by hand.

So if you want to rough up a pair of jeans at home, your options are a good sandpapering or hiring a laser gun. But if you opt for the laser, make sure you're not wearing the jeans at the time.

Which was the first-ever boy band?

It depends how far back you want to go.

Archaeologists have found that prehistoric hunters painted the sections of their caves that had the best acoustics for singing. We don't know exactly when groups started harmonising together, but we do know that ancient Greeks sang before they went into battle, that the Roman philosopher Seneca was kept up at night by practising choirs, and that, according to the Bible, hymns were sung at the Last Supper.

Singing together has long been important in religious ceremonies, so were the Christian brothers who performed Gregorian chants in the 9th century the first boy bands? Perhaps, but when people say 'boy bands', they are usually thinking more Monkees than monks, so let's look at some more recent releases.

The earliest direct ancestor of groups like BTS, the Jonas Brothers and One Direction is probably the Edison Quartet (later known as the Haydn Quartet). They were formed in 1896 to perform songs for Thomas Edison's company, Edison Records, and as they were part of the recording age, we think they can be considered a boy band. The founder members were John, Jere, Samuel and William, and they had hits including 'Put on Your Old Gray Bonnet', 'Will You Love Me in December as You Do in May?' and 'How'd You Like to Spoon with Me?'

So you could say that another of Thomas Edison's inventions was the boy band.

How do the umlauts change the pronunciation of Mötley Crüe?

They don't. Mötley Crüe's umlauts were intended to be purely decorative, to make the band look more European. They admitted they had no idea that umlauts changed the pronunciation, until they performed in Germany and the whole audience started chanting, 'Mutley Cruh, Mutley Cruh.'

Similarly, Motörhead's umlaut shouldn't alter the pronunciation of their name. When asked if Germans pronounced the band 'Moturhead', frontman Lemmy answered, 'No, they don't. I only put it in there to look mean.'

McDonald's used to put umlauts on their German menus. A Big Mac became a Big Mäc and a Filet-o-Fish was a Fishmäc. Sadly, the accents were dropped when they standardised their packaging around the world in 2007.

Spelling things incorrectly in songs – for example, Avril Lavigne's 'Sk8er Boi', Sinéad O'Connor's 'Nothing Compares 2 U' and Slade's 'Look Wot You Dun' – is called sensational spelling. Slade also had a hit with 'Coz I Luv You', which lead singer Noddy Holder said they chose as 'Because I Love You' looked a bit wet. They instead opted for a spelling that might 'be on toilet walls in the Midlands' to make it more hard-hitting. It went to No. 1, which Holder said gave them the courage of their convictions to keep their sensational spelling. Their future hits included 'Mama Weer All Crazee Now', 'Cum on Feel the Noize' and 'Skweeze Me, Pleeze Me'.

❯ Termites eat wood faster when listening to rock and heavy metal.

❯ A petition in 2016 to name the next heavy metal of the periodic table after Motörhead's Lemmy reached over 150,000 signatures.

❯ An analysis of over 22,000 heavy metal songs showed that 'burn' is the most metal word. The least metal word is 'particularly'.

❯ Wikipedia creator Jimmy Wales has said that his favourite Wiki page is the 'Metal Umlaut'.

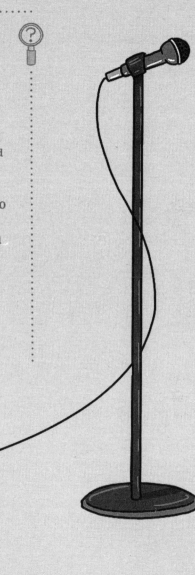

Why are sideburns called 'sideburns'?

. . . .

Ask Abraham Lincoln.

Sideburns get their name from an American military officer named General Ambrose Burnside (1824–81). They were originally called 'burnsides', but within a year the two halves of the word had been reversed, creating the modern version.

Burnside was by all accounts a charming and pleasant man. He was a talented inventor and created a gun called the Burnside carbine. (Its innovation was that it could be loaded at the back, saving soldiers the bother of putting the ammunition down the muzzle; this meant it was simple enough for mounted cavalry to use.) Despite his talents, he could be an ineffective general. After he took the blame for a battle that had gone badly wrong, President Lincoln told him he was the first man who'd been 'willing to relieve him of a particle of responsibility'. Burnside finally sent Lincoln his resignation letter on 15 April 1865 – the day the president was assassinated.

Lincoln was killed at the theatre while watching a comedy called *Our American Cousin*. The play featured a character called Lord Dundreary, who boasted a large pair of sideburns. He was so famous that before General Burnside came along, sideburns had been known as 'dundrearies'.

Other, earlier iterations included 'sidewhiskers' and 'muttonchops', although generally they're still known as sideburns today.

Why is laughter so infectious?

Humans evolved as social animals. We would hang out in groups, share resources and look after each other when times were tough. Today, if you want to join a group, you might ask if that seat is free, but before our ancestors learnt to speak, they needed to communicate in different ways. Laughter was a means of showing that you were not a threat and were up for a bit of fun; if the rest of the group started laughing along with you, then everyone could begin to relax.

It's not just laughter that can be caught from your friends; negative emotions can be catching too. A 2014 study of more than a billion Facebook posts found that people were more grumpy when the weather was bad, but also that if you're in sunny Sydney and have a number of friends in rainy Romford, you can 'catch' their bad mood.

······················· **HILARITY CLARITY** ·······················

❯ Two famous figures from ancient Greece are separately recorded as having died from laughter after seeing a donkey eating figs and drinking wine.

❯ In a 1686 treatise, clergyman Jean-Baptiste Thiers instructed people always to laugh discreetly, and never on workdays, Sundays, holy days or during Lent and Advent.

❯ There's a breed of cockerel from Indonesia whose crow sounds just like a human laugh. Until recently they could be owned only by the Indonesian royal family.

Can anything live without oxygen?

Every animal on the planet needs oxygen to survive – except for a tiny organism called *Henneguya salminicola*. It is part of a group of animals called myxozoans – sometimes nicknamed 'degenerate jellyfish' – which have no guts, no nervous system and no muscles. *Henneguya salminicola* gets all the energy it needs from the salmon it lives inside, and it has lost the power to breathe oxygen. It's the only multicellular animal ever observed that can get by without it.

All other multicellular organisms have structures in their cells called mitochondria, which turn oxygen into energy. There's one other family of animals, the loriciferans, who are thought to have no mitochondria, so they *might* live without oxygen, but studies are ongoing. Loriciferans live in the mud at the bottom of the ocean and also look like simple jellyfish. They could give clues as to what the very first animals on Earth were like, 500 million years ago; they may also be the kind of animals we might find on other planets where oxygen isn't in ready supply.

While no human can live without oxygen for very long, the nomadic Bajau people, who live along the coasts of Malaysia, the Philippines and Indonesia, can free-dive for 13 minutes at a time. Their ability to hold their breath underwater is genetic, as they have a DNA mutation which gives them larger spleens – 50% bigger than related groups who live much more of their lives on land. The spleen holds a stash of oxygenated red blood cells, and when you dive, it releases them into the bloodstream. Having a larger spleen means you can stay underwater for longer, saving on the price of scuba equipment.

How have dinosaur footprints survived for so long?

When you walk along a beach or nature trail, your footprints are usually quickly washed away or trodden over. This also happened to most dinosaur prints, but some have survived.

The conditions for them to leave a print had to be just right: the ground couldn't be too soft (or the dinosaur wouldn't leave a clear print), it couldn't be too hard (as it wouldn't have created an impression), and the print needed to be left undisturbed for long enough for it to start drying out in the Sun.

Once dried out, the surviving dinosaur footprints would need to be covered by pebbles, sand and earth, creating a protective layer. This would mean that not even thousands of new pairs of feet walking over the top or running water could destroy them. Over time this layer would erode, revealing the hidden footprint below.

Next time you're out for a walk, why not take a slight detour off the beaten path, and if you're lucky, your footprints could also be preserved for generations to come.

· DINO INFO ·

❯ In 2011, so many fossilised tracks were found at a single site in Arkansas that scientists suspect they were left by dinosaurs who had been stomping in the mud.

Can elephants sneeze?

Elephants clear their trunks in the same way that you clear your nose – by blowing through them. And as the trunk is a modified version of the nose, elephants can sneeze too.

An elephant's trunk is one of the most amazing organs in nature. It is incredibly strong, containing up to 40,000 muscles. Humans have a total of 600, but while our skeletal muscles are tethered to bones, elephants don't have any bones in their trunks, which means they move more like a human tongue.

Trunks are spacious inside, but they're also expandable: an elephant can dilate its nostrils and increase the trunk's volume by 64%. This means they can suck up five litres of water in under two seconds – although, as it's their nose, they have to squirt the water into their mouths in order to swallow it. When it comes to breathing, elephants can inhale air through their trunk at 336 mph – faster than a Japanese bullet train. Elephants can also use their trunks like a vacuum cleaner to hoover up food that is just out of their reach.

An African elephant research project, the 'Elephant Ethogram', has recorded 250 separate actions performed by a trunk: it can fulfil the role of a snorkel, trumpet, shower, comforter (baby elephants suck their trunks), food detector and much more. If the water in a drinking hole is muddy, elephants carefully use their trunks to siphon off the layer of clean water on the top. If an elephant needs to protect itself from the Sun, it will suck up dust and spray it over its own back. The very end of a trunk has 'fingers', which are used to pinch tiny objects. (This is one way of telling the difference between elephants: African elephants have two 'fingers', their

Asian cousins only one.) The same organ which can hoist a huge tree trunk can also pluck a single blade of grass.

In short, there is almost nothing an elephant can't do, as long as it has packed its trunk.

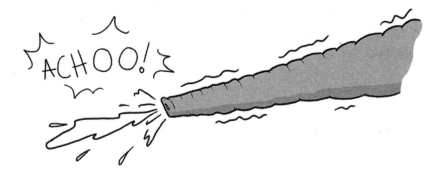

························· **NEVER FORGET** ························

❯ Elephants enjoy listening to a rumba, but not a tango.

❯ Elephants have a specific call they use to warn each other about bees.

❯ Elephants can catch yawns from humans with whom they are familiar.

❯ Wild elephants sleep for only two hours a day.

❯ A million large elephants weigh as much as a teaspoonful of neutron star.

❯ Elephants always walk on tiptoe.

How do cats know where they live?

Cats and humans have coexisted for a long time. They probably began living in close proximity when people started farming 10,000 years ago in the Middle East. Grain stores would have attracted rats and mice, so cats were allowed to hunt the rodents to prevent the crops from being ruined. In ancient Egypt, cats were worshipped, and the penalty for killing one was death. They were mummified when they died, and were accompanied by mummified mice for them to eat in the afterlife.

These days, many people enjoy having felines as companions, and cats like, or tolerate, living with humans. They know where their base is, because that's where they get shelter, food and social interaction, but each cat will also establish a wider territory. This would have been their hunting ground when they were wild animals, before they became domesticated and kept as pets.

For a timid cat, this territory might be the 10-square-metre area around their cat flap, but for others it could be a square kilometre. They mark their territories by rubbing the scent glands in their faces on planters, posts and trees, by scratching – which also leaves their scent – and with urine and poo. Cats have an excellent sense of smell and can tell both where they've been and when they were there. They can also follow this scent trail back home.

Scent marking also lets other cats in the area know they're there. Cats in urban areas often have overlapping territories, but as they are solitary creatures, they patrol their territories at different times of the day. This doesn't always work, and you might have heard the resulting catfight when the rota system fails.

· **CLAWS FOR THOUGHT** ·

❯ Cats spend about 70% of their time sleeping.

❯ A US study found that atheists are more likely to have a cat than regular church-goers.

How does a chameleon change colour?

For centuries, chameleons have been famous for their ability to change colour, but it wasn't until 2015 that scientists worked out how they do it. It had been assumed that, like other colour-changing creatures such as octopuses and cuttlefish, their skin cells contained sacs of pigment which could be released when required. In fact, their skin has special cells that contain crystals, which work like a selective mirror: when light bounces off them, they reflect different colours. By either tightening or relaxing their skin, they alter the spacing between these cells, and this changes the colour they reflect.

These crystals are also the reason for a chameleon's usual colour. The pigment in their skin is actually yellow, but the crystals underneath reflect blue light, which mixes with the yellow pigment to make green – which is useful most of the time because it camouflages them in their leafy environment.

Contrary to popular belief, chameleons change colour to stand out from their surroundings, not blend into them. Only the males do it, turning from green to yellow, orange or red, usually to attract a female or intimidate a rival. When they get excited, the tiny crystals in their skin rattle around and are pushed further away from each other. As the distance between them grows, the colours you see bouncing from the chameleon's skin change, going from yellow to orange and then red. If you wanted to ruin a chameleon's reputation as it attempted to show off, you could press down on its skin while it was turning red. This would compact the crystals again and change it back to green.

While the crystals are key to how chameleons usually change colour, they do have some pigment in their body. Like us, their skin can get darker due to melanin, which also helps them to warm up, since dark colours absorb more heat. Or it can be a sign of submission: if they've made themselves bright red to scare off a love rival, then suddenly realise that their competitor is bigger than they are, they might use melanin to quickly turn themselves a dull brown to show they are withdrawing their interest.

How do bees become queen bees?

There are three types of honeybees: drones (male bees), workers (female bees who can't reproduce) and queens (fertile female bees). Unfertilised bee eggs turn into drones, while fertilised eggs can become either workers or queens, depending on what they eat. When the bee larvae hatch, they are known as 'grubs' and are all initially fed on royal jelly. This is also called 'bee milk' and is produced by glands in the worker bees' heads. Packed with proteins, carbohydrates and vitamins, it helps the young bees grow.

After a few days, most of the grubs are switched to a new diet of bee bread, a mixture of partially fermented pollen, honey and bee saliva. This is high in energy, but also contains plant chemicals that prevent the ovaries from developing properly in the bees that eat it.

The queens-to-be continue to be fed exclusively on royal jelly. By staying on their original diet and not being exposed to the plant chemicals, they develop into queens with fully functioning ovaries, becoming the only bees able to lay fertilised eggs and keep the hive going for another generation.

Can you get princess bees?

Only if you look at their family trees.

Although multiple queens may be developing at once, there can be only one. The first queen to emerge from her cell will quickly destroy all the others. If two queens emerge at the same time, they will emit piping and tooting sounds, before fighting to the death.

Often new queens are reared while the old one is still alive. After they emerge, a queen will swarm, leaving with some workers and drones to start a new colony, or the hive will dispose of the old queen in favour of a younger, more productive one.

Technically, since all the bees in the hive are the children of the queen, you could argue that all the females are princesses. After hatching, all the non-queen females become workers, doing everything from collecting pollen to maintaining the hive to looking after the queen, before eventually dying from exhaustion. It's not a particularly regal lifestyle.

. . . . HIVE MIND . . . .

❯ Bees sometimes fill their stomachs with water and regurgitate it into their own nest. When it evaporates, it acts as a kind of air-conditioning.

If the monarch has firstborn twins, how is it decided who is next in line for the throne?

In Britain, it's exactly what you'd expect: the first down the royal birth canal is also first in line for the throne. That said, the younger sibling may still take the throne. James II of Scotland – insensitively nicknamed James of the Fiery Face due to his large red birthmark – was a second-born twin. In 1437, his older brother died, and James became king at the tender age of six.

Most twins don't come down the birth canal at all. 60% of twins in the UK are born by caesarean. For a royal birth, this would mean the obstetrician could theoretically end up choosing the future king or queen.

Princess Charlene of Monaco delivered twins by C-section in 2014, with Princess Gabriella born two minutes before her brother, Prince Jacques. Nonetheless, Jacques will inherit the throne from his father because, under Monaco's succession laws, a male sibling always takes precedence. This was the case in Britain until 2013, when, just before the Duchess of Cambridge gave birth to her first child, the Succession to the Crown Act was passed, which allowed firstborn daughters to inherit the throne. They needn't have rushed: in the end, she gave birth to a boy.

Perhaps it would be fairer for twins to rule together, but history suggests this isn't always the best idea. From 1076 to 1082, twin brothers, confusingly called Ramon Berenguer II and Berenguer Ramon II, ruled Catalonia jointly. Ramon Berenguer's reign was cut short when he was killed in a supposed hunting accident. However, it was assumed that his brother had had him assassinated, and to this day he's known as Berenguer Ramon II the Fratricide. Ramon Berenguer got his own back posthumously: his son inherited the throne. The son, of course, was called Ramon Berenguer III.

· GAME OF KNOWNS ·

❯ For the Queen's Diamond Jubilee in 2012, Marks & Spencer made a special Colin the Caterpillar cake, complete with chocolate crown.

❯ Edward VI had servants test his chamber pot to make sure it wasn't covered in poison.

❯ Identical twins aren't very good at telling their own faces apart.

❯ The phenomenon of twins developing a language that only they can understand is called cryptophasia.

Why was Queen Elizabeth crowned Elizabeth II when there was more than one Queen Elizabeth before her?

It's true that there were several Queen Elizabeths before Elizabeth II. There were two in the 1400s alone: Elizabeth Woodville, the wife of Edward IV, and Elizabeth of York, who became queen when she married Henry VII. More recently, Elizabeth Bowes-Lyon was queen between 1936 and 1952, when her husband George VI held the throne.

However, because they were married to a king, these Elizabeths were queen consorts rather than heads of state. Monarchs who rule in their own right, such as Elizabeth II, are queens regnant and are the only ones to be given a number.

Other types of queen include queen dowagers; this is the title for a queen consort who has outlived her husband when a new head of state is crowned. If a queen dowager is also the mother of the reigning monarch, as Elizabeth II's mother was, then she is known as the queen mother.

There are also queen regents, a title given if a king is abroad for a long time and decides to hand over power to his wife. This honour is fairly rare but was granted to Catherine of Aragon and Catherine Parr when Henry VIII was out of the country.

If you fancy being a queen yourself but don't have any royal connections, we might have a solution for you. Piel Island, off the coast of Cumbria, claims its own monarchy separate from the British one: whoever runs the local pub, the

Ship Inn, gets to style themself as the King or Queen of Piel Island. The positions were previously held by Queen Sheila and King Steve, but they left in May 2021, so the island is on the hunt for a new royal family.

· QUEEN-EALOGY ·

❯ In 2015, a slice of Queen Elizabeth II's wedding cake sold for £500. Its alcohol content meant that after 68 years, it was still deemed edible.

❯ Between 1986 and 1991, the Queen's annual Christmas message was produced by David Attenborough.

❯ When in London, Queen Louise of Sweden always carried a card saying, 'I am the Queen of Sweden' in case she was hit by a bus.

❯ Queen guitarist Brian May has released a cologne that smells of badgers.

Why do you wait for a bus, then three come at once?

There's an explanation for this phenomenon, which is known as 'bus bunching'.

If a bus is delayed for any reason, then by the time it reaches its next stop there will be more people than usual waiting. This requires the driver to spend more time letting everyone on, which means the bus will be even later by the time it reaches its next stop, where the same thing will have happened, and this will continue around the route.

Meanwhile, the bus behind the delayed one will find its stops emptier (because the waiting passengers caught the earlier delayed bus), so it will travel through the city more quickly than expected and gain on the original bus.

To combat this problem, bus companies build additional slack into their systems – such as extra buses and longer scheduled travel times – in order to provide a steady service.

Who invented speed cameras?

They were created by racing driver Maurice Gatsonides, who wanted to increase his lap times. His device measured how long it took him to travel between two wires and then calculated his speed.

Gatsonides later sold his invention to the police. The cameras – known as 'Gatsos' – are still in use, although the detection wires have been upgraded and systems now also use radars and lasers.

Not even being caught by his own device could put a damper on Gatsonides' need for speed. 'I am often caught by my own speed cameras and find hefty fines on my doormat,' he said. 'Even I can't escape my own invention because I love speeding.'*

* The QI Elves do not condone this behaviour; we always ride our bicycles while respecting the speed limit.

Do we drive on the left because right-handed knights on horseback wanted to tackle oncoming rivals with their strong hand?

This seems to be the most likely explanation, although on its website the AA suggests an alternative theory: it might have allowed medieval riders to offer each other the hand of friendship as they passed. If that's true, then ye olde M25 must have been a much calmer place than it is today.

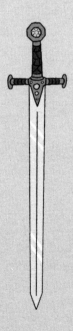

What's the difference between a ship and a boat?

There is no easy way to answer this without getting into a row. According to the *Oxford English Dictionary*, boats are usually small, open vessels (so there's no 'above deck' or 'below deck') powered by oars, a sail or an engine. Traditionally, ships are much larger, sailing across open seas, while boats usually stay close to shore or make short hops across the sea. Another popular rule of thumb holds that generally a ship can carry a boat (such as a lifeboat), but a boat can't carry a ship.

There's a lot of overlap, so none of these definitions is watertight. For example, the *OED* definition of 'boats' says it also includes some larger vessels, such as ferries. However, ferries have above- and below-deck areas, and they carry lifeboats, meaning that logically they should be ships. Large fishing boats have the same exceptions and frequently go out to sea for long periods, so why are they boats? Not only that, some rowing boats – surely among the boatiest boats of all – are affectionately nicknamed 'ships' by their owners. As for the 'a ship can't be carried' rule, there are some enormous vessels that hoist and transport huge container ships, meaning that they are ships that are literally *designed* to be able to carry a ship.

Even more confusingly, naval convention has declared that submarines should be known as 'boats', despite being entirely below deck and operating in the open sea. Harder to fathom still, the Royal Navy gives its submarines the prefix 'HMS', standing for 'Her Majesty's Ship'. Balloons, planes and spacecraft can also be known as 'ships' (hence 'spaceship'),

although none of these should be confused with a 'ship of the desert', which is a poetic way of describing a camel.

It gets even worse when you read further down in the *OED* and discover that 'boat' can also be a colloquial term for 'a large ocean-going ship'. The word 'ship', on the other hand, was traditionally used to refer to a small container for incense, otherwise known as – you guessed it – an 'incense boat'.

When the *Guardian* looked into this, one correspondent summed it up rather neatly, writing, 'A ship's captain gets annoyed if you refer to his vessel as a boat, but a boat's captain does not get annoyed if you refer to his vessel as a ship.'

It's worth pointing out that the British vessel known as *Boaty McBoatface* is a submarine, and therefore – by naval custom, at least – actually is a boat.

How do ships get their names?
The Royal Navy's ships were usually named after members of royalty or places in England, but following the 1707 Act of Union two ships were hurriedly renamed *Edinburgh* and *Glasgow*. Naming moved away from geographical labels, and ships began to be given names that were felt to reflect the idea of 'Britishness', like *Conqueror*, *Dreadnaught*, *Hero*, *Illustrious* and *Superb*. Captured French ships that were added to the fleet were often given an anglicised version of the original French name – partly to annoy the French navy.

As the Royal Navy grew, it began to run out of names and now often reuses names as ships leave service. One of the names which has been reused several times is HMS *Victory*. While some ships with this moniker have been successful and gone on to a happy retirement, the third HMS *Victory* was damaged by an accidental fire and broken up, while the fourth was wrecked in 1744 – just seven years after it was built.

What did the person who named New South Wales have against North Wales?

Europeans discovered New South Wales thanks to a scientist who was trying to measure the size of the Solar System. Astronomer Edmund Halley (of comet fame) had worked out that it could be calculated by measuring how long it took Venus to move across the face of the Sun, but anyone wishing to do so needed measurements from 76 specific locations across the globe. One of these was the South Pacific, so in 1769 Captain James Cook set sail for Tahiti with a crew and some telescopes.

The expedition was planned by scientists at the Royal Society, but Cook was also set a secret mission by the Admiralty. After the measurements had been made, he was to search between Tahiti and New Zealand for a 'Continent or Land of great extent'. In the 1600s, Dutch explorers had mapped the north, west and south coasts of Australia, as well as Tasmania and New Zealand, but they didn't know what lay between them. In 1770, Cook discovered the east coast of Australia and claimed it for Britain.

He originally called the land New Wales, but soon changed the name to New South Wales. It could be that the coastline reminded him of the Welsh coast, or it could just have been Wales's turn: there were already islands in the South Pacific named New Britain, New Ireland and New Hebrides, and Cook later named another group of islands New Caledonia – the Roman name for Scotland.

The Dutch also sometimes named their discoveries as 'New' versions of a European area. New Zealand is named after the Dutch province of Zeeland, and Australia was previously known as New Holland. In North America, New York City was previously called New Amsterdam.

Although we don't know why South Wales was chosen ahead of North Wales on the Australian map, there was a New North Wales in Canada, along with a second New South Wales. Canada also had a New South-West Wales, which, confusingly, was to the east of New South Wales. The Canadian version of New South Wales remained on the map from 1612 to 1865, a total of 253 years. Since the Australian New South Wales was given its name in 1770, 251 years ago, it still has a couple of years before it overtakes Canada as the longest-running New South Wales.

. . . .

How was Venus used to work out the size of the Solar System?
By looking at how the planets moved across the night sky, astronomers had long been able to calculate their relative distances from the Sun, but not the exact size of the gap between them. Halley worked out that when Venus passed in front of the Sun (known as a 'transit'), observers at different latitudes on Earth would see this event at different angles, and it would appear to last for a slightly different amount of time. Using geometry, he would then be able to triangulate the distance from Earth to Venus, and from there work out the distances to the other planets.

Halley died in 1742, before any transit occurred. When the experiment was finally carried out, the distance from the Earth to the Sun was measured to be 95 million miles. Modern measurements put it at 92.9 million, which, given the complexity of the experiment, means that figuratively the original calculation wasn't a million miles away.

Why are New York's taxis yellow?

New York's first taxis were imported from France and were decked out in red and green. The taxi business then expanded, with fleets choosing colours to distinguish themselves from their competitors. You could find red ones, yellow ones, black ones, brown and white ones, chequered ones, and in *The Great Gatsby* Myrtle is described as watching four cars go past before choosing one which is 'lavender-coloured with grey upholstery'.

One of the sources for yellow taxis was the appropriately named Yellow Cab Company in Chicago, which later expanded to other cities, including NYC. It was operated by John Hertz (of car-rental fame), who is said to have got the idea from a local university study which found that yellow was the best choice because it was the most visible to potential passengers looking for a cab on a busy street. Hertz wasn't the first to choose yellow for his fleet; that was a businessman called Albert Rockwell, who owned the Yellow Taxicab Company. He chose the colour because it was his wife's favourite.

By the late 1950s, New York's taxis had settled on a range of oranges, golds and yellows, before committing to a very specific colour in 1967: Dupont M6284 yellow.

Do cabs in New York come in any colours other than yellow?

Yes. Private hires, like Uber, come in a variety of colours, and as the demand for yellow cabs far exceeds supply, in the early 2010s the city introduced a fleet of taxis that mostly operate in the outer boroughs. They're known as 'boro taxis', and they are light green.

Why is New York called 'the Big Apple'?

Calling NYC 'the Big Apple' was popularised in the 1920s, when sports writer John J. FitzGerald wrote a horse-racing column called 'Around the Big Apple'. FitzGerald wrote, 'The Big Apple. The dream of every lad that ever threw a leg over a thoroughbred and the goal of all horsemen. There's only one Big Apple. That's New York.' He's said to have picked up the phrase from two African American stable hands he overheard at a racecourse in New Orleans talking about heading for a big prize – the big apple – and used the name for his column.

In the 1970s, the nickname was adopted by the tourism board, replacing New York's previous nickname, 'Fun City'. Then, in 1997, the south-west corner of Broadway and West 54th Street, where FitzGerald used to live, was renamed Big Apple Corner. If you've ever wondered whether apples have corners, now you know where to find the biggest one.

Which US state has the best nickname?
New York is the Empire State, but some of our other favourites include Louisiana, which is the Pelican State, Utah, the Beehive State, Montana, the Treasure State, and Missouri, which is the 'Show Me' State.

Where is Shangri-La?

Shangri-La – a name for a remote paradise – started out as a completely fictional place, first appearing in a book published nearly a century ago. Now this previously mythical spot has become a real place you can visit. A region called Zhongdian, part of Yunnan province, in south-west China, renamed itself Shangri-La County in 2001, largely to promote tourism to the area.

Shangri-La has also been given to a range of luxury hotels, and strangely, the man who coined the word also shares his name with a hotel brand. James Hilton, the English journalist who wrote about it in the 1933 story *Lost Horizon*, described Shangri-La as a mysterious Tibetan valley. According to some sources, he based his idea of Shangri-La on *National Geographic* articles written by a botanist who had visited China's Yunnan and Sichuan provinces. If this is true, then the place Hilton was using as inspiration – Yunnan – contains the area that ended up renaming itself Shangri-La for tourism purposes. So perhaps the name fits.

Hilton's book was so popular, and the idea of Shangri-La so enticing, that as well as the hotel chain, the US president's rural retreat in Maryland was also named Shangri-La. It was given the name by Franklin D. Roosevelt in 1942; a decade later, President Eisenhower renamed it Camp David, after his grandson.

Rock, paper or scissors?

Paper, if it's the first round. People have a slight preference for rock as their opening play, men especially, so paper is a sensible place to start. Unless they've read this book, in which case they'll probably go for paper, so you should choose scissors. Although now we've said that, perhaps it's worth trying rock.

After that, you can utilise a bit of psychology to give yourself the edge. A 2014 Chinese study found that after playing a winning move, such as picking rock and beating scissors, people tend to stick with the same shape in the next round, meaning they'll probably play rock again. However, when they lose, they tend to shake things up and try something different. This is referred to as a 'win–stay, lose–shift' strategy, and you can use it to try to predict your opponent's next move.

If you want to get in some practice against an easy opponent, you could start with a chimpanzee. Japanese scientists were able to teach chimps the game, and by the end of training they were about as good at playing as a four-year-old human. It did take 100 days for them to learn the rules, so maybe try to find an ape that's already mastered them.

If you want a challenge, you could try a really difficult opponent. The University of Tokyo has built a robot that has a 100% success rate against humans. It uses a high-speed camera to detect what shape its opponent's hand is about to make, and a fraction of a second later plays the move to beat it.

Where does the Rock, Paper, Scissors game come from?
There isn't one widely accepted origin story, and indeed the

game may have developed along several different paths. There are depictions of 'finger flashing' games on the wall of an Egyptian tomb from 2000 BC and on ancient Japanese scrolls.

There are many different versions of the game around the world. In Indonesia, they have a human, an ant and an elephant (the elephant squashes the human, the human crushes the ant, and the ant beats the elephant by crawling up its trunk and nibbling its brain). One ancient version involves a frog, which can beat a slug, a slug, which can beat a snake, and a snake, which can beat a frog. No, we're not sure how a slug could beat a snake either.

· ONE MORE ROUND ·

❯ In 2005, Christie's and Sotheby's held a Rock, Paper, Scissors match to decide who would auction off a client's $20 million art collection. Christie's won with scissors.

❯ An annual United States of America Rock, Paper, Scissors Championship used to be held in Las Vegas, with a prize of $50,000 for the winner. Sadly, it has now folded.

Why do ice-hockey players fight so much?

....

They don't. At least, not as much as they used to.

Thirty years ago, fighting was part and parcel of North America's National Hockey League. Famous brawls such as the Good Friday Massacre or the St Patrick's Day Massacre were even celebrated by fans. In 1980, there was an average of more than one big brawl per game, but by 2019 it was less than one fight in every five, and the numbers continue to fall.

This change is largely due to the punishment for fighting being increased, as the league works on improving its image. To avoid fines and suspensions, teams have stopped employing an 'enforcer' – the player whose sole job was to start fights. They would deliberately target the opposing team's best player or try to disrupt their opponents' concentration when they were on a roll.

The most literal hockey 'enforcer' was a KGB agent who turned out for the Soviet Union against the USA in 1980. He had been travelling with the team to stop anyone from defecting, and whenever the Soviet team looked certain to win, he was allowed to play. When he was tackled by a US player, his shirt rode up to reveal a hidden gun.

Ice hockey has always been violent. The very first recorded indoor match in 1875 ended in a fight after some boys jumped onto the ice mid-match and one was struck across the head. It seems that the group might have arrived early for their allotted time on the ice or the match overran, but either way, Kingston, Ontario's *Daily British Whig* reported that 'shins and heads were battered, benches smashed and the lady spectators fled in confusion'.

Many people blamed toxic masculinity for hockey violence, but it was not confined to the men's game. The first women's ice-hockey game to be played in New York was between the St Nicholas Blues and the Manhattan Reds, in 1917. An article about it reported, 'Of course there were several bumps, tosses and falls, but no serious damage was reported, only that Miss Ruth Denesha had a couple of teeth loosened.'

While North American and Soviet teams have often had games cancelled or postponed due to fighting, things are a little more genteel in Britain: in 2020, a game between Peterborough Phantoms and Telford Tigers was delayed because the referee had forgotten his trousers.

Why do we call it a 'derby'?

The first derby was in 1780, when the 12th Earl of Derby wanted to race horses with his friends. The fields at Epsom Downs provided a suitable venue, and the winner of the earl's first race was his own horse, Bridget. Over the next few years, the race increased in fame, and people began to call it 'the Derby'. Fast-forward a few decades, and Victorians started referring to large sporting fixtures with high stakes as 'derbies'.

We also have local derbies, which are matches between two teams from the same area. Though coined in 1909, well after the original horse-racing event, the current Earl of Derby (the 19th) says it too comes from his family's name, believing that the moniker might have stemmed from two local rugby league teams, St Helens and Wigan, who compete in the Wigan–Saints derby. The term 'local' is slightly confusing here because, despite being called the Earl of Derby and having a horse race in Surrey, the earl's ancestral home is in Knowsley, Liverpool. St Helens and Wigan first started playing rugby against each other on the outskirts of the Earl of Derby's estate, so this may be the true origin of 'derby day'.

Why do we say someone is 'toadying'?

A 'toady' comes from the days of quack doctors in the 17th and 18th centuries, when charlatans would create and sell drinks that supposedly worked as an antidote for poisoning. Their assistants were employed to eat (or pretend to eat) a toad, before feigning sickness and drinking the magical tonic. To the astonishment of the watching crowd, they would be miraculously cured.

Unsurprisingly, the practice of swallowing live toads was considered servile and low, and that's why we call someone who is being sycophantic a 'toady'.

How can some people walk slowly across hot coals, but it really hurts if I accidentally touch a shelf in the oven for a split second?

Actually, it's not that hard to walk short distances across hot coals. They're not made of real coal; they are charcoal – highly heated wood – and charcoal conducts heat very badly. The word 'conducts' is important. Conduction is one of the basic ways in which heat is transmitted: when two surfaces touch each other, hot molecules (which vibrate a lot) bang into colder molecules and transfer energy to them, meaning they heat up. But because the molecules in each material are different, they conduct heat at different speeds. Most metals can transfer heat several thousand times faster than charcoal.

When you walk on hot coals, your feet absorb *some* heat from the surface, but not enough to burn you at first. At normal walking pace, with only about half a second of contact per step, you shouldn't feel any burning (for a while at least). Of course, if you walk too far, your feet will eventually heat up enough to burn your skin. But most people can walk safely along about 5 metres of embers, with a surface temperature of about 540°C, before their feet start to blister. (It's important the right charcoal is used too: some woods burn at higher temperatures, meaning your feet will blister quicker.)

Metal, on the other hand, is a brilliant conductor of heat, meaning that when you touch the shelf in a hot oven, it swiftly transfers huge amounts of heat to your finger and burns you. This is why pan handles were traditionally made of wood, not metal; it's also why very few people walk barefoot along 540°C metal surfaces.

One last tip: if you ever *do* have to walk on hot coals, don't run, as that will push your feet further into the coals and could mean that the top of your feet get burnt. And remember, fire-walking can go badly wrong. In Australia in 2002, twenty KFC staff on the last day of a management course were hospitalised for burns after trying fire-walking. *The Age* newspaper ran the story under the headline, 'KFC Bosses Aren't Chicken, But They Sure Are Tender'.

Why do some people get bitten by mosquitoes, while others get away scot-free?

When it comes to mosquitoes, about one person in five is a 'high attractor type', meaning they really get it in the neck (and any other areas of exposed skin). If you fall into this category, there isn't much you can do about it as 85% of our susceptibility to mosquito bites is down to genetic factors. Your biteability depends on the following:

Blood type

Mosquitoes land on people with type O blood twice as often as people with type A. Additionally, 85% of people give off a chemical signal through their skin that indicates their blood type. Mosquitoes bite more people who give off the signal than those who don't, regardless of their actual blood type.

Breath

Mosquitoes can smell carbon dioxide from 160 feet away. Larger people exhale more of it as a rule, which makes them more attractive to mosquitoes. This is why children often go unbitten, while their parents suffer.

Bacteria

Mozzies seem to like the composition of some people's skin bacteria. They're also drawn to ammonia, lactic acid and uric acid – chemicals that we naturally excrete via our skin and breath.

Booze

Mosquitoes are more likely to land on people who have been drinking than those who haven't.

Black clothes

Mosquitoes fly close to the ground and look for targets who stand out against the horizon. Darker colours are more obvious, so if you're in dark clothing, you're likely to be spotted and bitten. Moving around helps make you more visible to them too, as their vision is partly based on movement.

Babies

Mosquitoes really like pregnant women, as not only do they tend to exhale more carbon dioxide, they also have a slightly higher body temperature.

So, to avoid mosquito bites, the best thing to do is wear a white tracksuit, stand still, and don't breathe or have a drink. And try to have the right blood type, if at all possible, and not be pregnant. Alternatively, if you have a friend who breathes heavily, wears black, drinks like a fish and has type O blood, then stick with them and you probably won't need any protection at all.

Why is yawning contagious?

Yawning is one big mystery. The average adult yawns 20 times per day, but we still don't know for sure why we do it. We yawn when we're tired, but also when we're stressed: professional athletes do it before high-pressure sporting events. Foetuses yawn in the womb, before they can even breathe.

The scientific study of yawning is called chasmology and goes back over 2,500 years to the ancient Greek physician Hippocrates. Today, a popular theory is that a yawn is a 'catch-up' breath that happens when you're tired, because you're not working as hard at breathing as you should. You are short on oxygen coming in and have too much toxic carbon dioxide building up in your lungs. Yawning may cool down the brain, to perk it up and make it work a bit faster.

It could also be a way of communicating that we're bored, anxious or tired. This could explain why yawns are catching: humans copy each other all the time when communicating – be it laughing together or altering our body language to mirror a friend. If this is true, then it could explain why people who have psychopathic personalities have been proven to be less likely to catch a yawn, since they typically have less empathy.

You can even catch a yawn from yourself: just sitting around *thinking* about yawning can cause you to actually yawn. Bearing that in mind, please do not read this while driving or operating heavy machinery.

Why does my voice sound so different when I hear it on a recording?

When you listen to your own voice on a recording, the sound waves strike your eardrum, which begins to vibrate. This vibration then travels to three smaller bones in your ear – the malleus, incus and stapes (also known as the hammer, anvil and stirrup) – which amplify the vibrations and send them to your spiral-shaped cochlea. The cochlea is filled with liquid and 25,000 nerve endings that interpret the vibrations and send signals to your brain, which interprets them as sound.

But when you're actually speaking, the sound of your voice travels through the solid matter of your skull, which makes it appear deeper, louder and more resonant. This means that while a recorded version of your voice might sound higher-pitched to you, to everyone else that is how you always sound.

If you're listening to the audio book, please imagine my voice sounding slightly lower. It sounds great in my head.

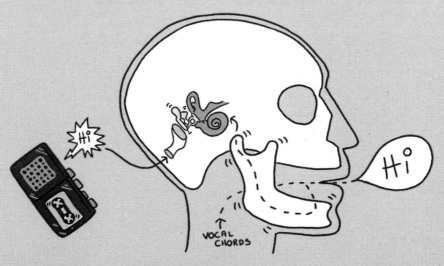

Why do artists make self-portraits?

Dutch painter Vincent van Gogh dedicated the latter half of his life's work to bright sunflowers, dreamlike landscapes and poignant self-portraits – subject matter that was either very cheap or free to view. Between 1886 and 1889, he produced more than 30 self-portraits, partly due to a lack of commissions and partly because he couldn't pay an artist's model for their time. It wasn't always easy. As he wrote to his brother, Theo: 'They say – and I am willing to believe it – that it is difficult to know yourself – but it isn't easy to paint yourself either.'

Sometimes it's hard for the contemporary viewer to feel an affinity with figures from the past, but perhaps in Van Gogh's case his posthumous popularity and his place in the collective psyche can be traced to the many ways he captured himself on canvas and created a lasting connection between artist and viewer. Not only do self-portraits capture how an artist saw themselves, they're also important records of how they wanted to be perceived. Seventeenth-century Italian painter Artemisia Gentileschi often used her own face when painting female figures, such as in her *Self Portrait as Saint Catherine of Alexandria*. Exceptionally for the period, Gentileschi's figures are portrayed from a woman's perspective, and she lets them take centre-stage, often depicting them as physically and emotionally strong.

Arguably more popular than ever – with the invention of mobile phones ushering in the era of the 'selfie' – self-portraits have stood the test of time.

What makes modern art, art?

It's important first to make sure that what you're looking at isn't actually *contemporary* art. There is quite a debate over modern art's timeline, but it generally ranges from late-1800s Impressionism – colourful, light-filled scenes painted outdoors rather than in a studio – up until the 1960s, incorporating movements such as conceptual art, where the idea or concept behind the piece is as significant as the work itself. Anything made since the 1960s usually gets the label 'contemporary', not 'modern'.

Regardless of when an artwork was made, though you might not think of it as 'art', it could be that it's just not your cup of tea. Few of today's art lovers would complain that Claude Monet's work 'isn't real art', but he came under heavy criticism when he began painting 'impressions' of the everyday scenes before him. Impressionism was a move away from the academic art – planned and precise, and often portraying known subject matter – that preceded it. Just as contemporary art provokes debate, Monet's critics argued that his work was an uncontrolled, unfinished mess.

Art – whether that's painting, sculpture, dance, literature or music – is meant to make you think. If that thought is, 'That's not art,' then it's important to question *why* you think that. As the viewer, you fulfil the artwork's purpose simply by being there, and every person will think something slightly different. Ask yourself, do you think the creator intended you to feel this way? What would you change? What makes something art?

Wouldn't life be monotonous if we never wondered 'why'?

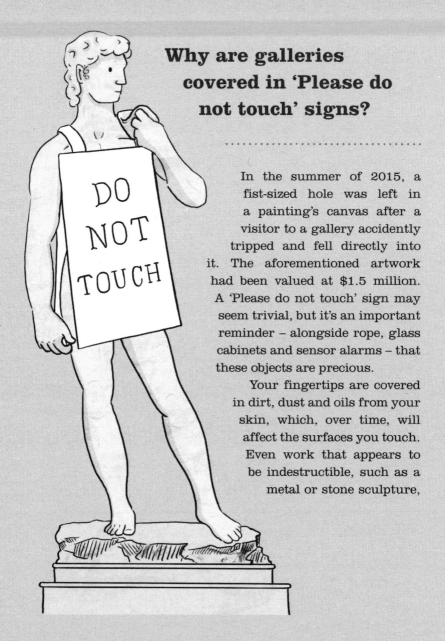

Why are galleries covered in 'Please do not touch' signs?

In the summer of 2015, a fist-sized hole was left in a painting's canvas after a visitor to a gallery accidentally tripped and fell directly into it. The aforementioned artwork had been valued at $1.5 million. A 'Please do not touch' sign may seem trivial, but it's an important reminder – alongside rope, glass cabinets and sensor alarms – that these objects are precious.

Your fingertips are covered in dirt, dust and oils from your skin, which, over time, will affect the surfaces you touch. Even work that appears to be indestructible, such as a metal or stone sculpture, will eventually start to show signs of damage. In 2009, the Ashmolean Museum in Oxford opened a 'Conserving the Past' gallery, which included a machine called the 'Touchometer'. One half was protected in glass, while the other was left exposed. Visitors were invited to touch the uncovered side as many times as they liked, and each interaction was counted and added to a running total to highlight the cumulative effect. By 2015, the counter had hit 8 million interactions, and a clear difference had emerged between the covered, preserved side and the visibly damaged half that had been left exposed to visitors' contacts. The machine was eventually touched so many times that it broke and had to be sent for refurbishment.

Visitors do like to engage with exhibits, and some museums now have tours and displays specifically designed with this in mind. Art exhibitions can include sculptures you're encouraged to walk on, light installations you alter with your shadow and performance art you can be a part of. What mustn't change, though, is the opportunity for people to see the many rare and significant objects that can't survive grubby fingers and visitor interaction, and the signs you see in front of them play an important part in helping to conserve them for the next generation to enjoy.

Why do we have finger and toenails?

We can get a clue from the other animals with nails, such as monkeys, chimpanzees and orang-utans. They tend to use their nails to provide grip when climbing and to hold on tightly to objects. Mammals with claws instead of nails can't manipulate small objects nearly as well.

Toenails also provide protection for vitally important body parts. Human feet contain lots of nerve endings, which meant that in the days before shoes, people could feel where they were walking and safely negotiate unfamiliar ground. And even today, our toes are particularly important for balance: people who lose them often report that it takes them a while to adjust to their new gait. Imagine how much it hurts when you stub your toe; it would be a lot more painful if you didn't have a nail functioning as a mini toe-helmet.

Do fingernails keep growing after you die?

This is a popular myth. Your fingernails grow from a pocket in the nail bed called the matrix, gaining 0.1 mm in length every day. This process cannot continue after death, but what does sometimes happen is that dehydration and drying cause the skin around the fingernails to retract. This can make them look slightly longer, even though they haven't actually grown at all.

· NAILED IT ·

❯ In 2018, Shridhar Chillal, the man with the longest fingernails in the world, cut them off after 66 years of growth. He grew them only on his left hand, but the combined length was a whopping 909.6 cm.

Who first thought it would be a good idea to put a lens on your eye rather than in your glasses?

Leonardo da Vinci is sometimes credited with inventing the contact lens in 1508, but the truth is a little blurrier.

His notebooks describe an experiment whereby a person might put their head into a bowl of water, which would refract the light rays and allow them to see their own shoulders. This is not a contact lens as we know it, of course, but it is the first step towards improving your eyesight by bending light. Though as the Royal College of Optometrists has observed, it wouldn't have been wildly successful because of the risk of drowning.

Contact lenses like the ones we know today first appeared in 1801, when English scientist Thomas Young placed quarter-inch-long (0.6 cm) water-filled tubes in front of subjects' eyes. The only problem was that they had to be stuck to their eyeballs with wax or mounted in a metallic ring to prevent the water from spilling out.

Lenses made out of glass appeared in 1887. Despite being individually fitted to patients' eyes, they were extremely uncomfortable. Wearers experienced a huge amount of pain after just a few hours because the lenses cut off the oxygen supply from the air to the eyes.

Today, lenses are made of soft plastics with a high water content that let oxygen through to the eye, making them more comfortable to wear. So, if you're still gluing test tubes to your eyeballs, it might be time to book an appointment at the opticians.

Why don't my eyes steam up like my glasses do?

If you open up your dishwasher after a cycle and peer inside, you will find that your spectacles quickly fog up. This is because some of the steam from the machine lands on the cold surface of the glass and turns into tiny droplets of liquid water.

Luckily, your body has a few tricks to stop this from happening to your eyes. The first is that your eyes are never as cold as your glasses. They have a blood supply that keeps them warm – something which is lacking in your glasses – and the colder a surface is, the more likely it is that any water vapour landing on it will cool down and turn into droplets.

Secondly, your eyes contain an anti-fog agent. Anti-fog agents were invented by NASA after Eugene Cernan, the second American to do a spacewalk, almost died when his helmet fogged up and he found himself unable to get back into his ship. Astronauts today use high-tech chemicals and gels to stop things steaming up, but your anti-fog agent is much simpler: it's your tears, which work simply by moistening the surface of your eye, preventing fogging. It's the same reason a mirror in your bathroom won't steam up if it's covered in water.

Finally, if all else fails and your eyesight is still a little blurry due to the steam, you can just blink. Blinking acts like a set of windscreen wipers, removing tears or fog so you can see clearly once again.

Why do we rub our eyes when we're tired?

Tired eyes are often dry eyes, and rubbing them stimulates the body to produce tears, which moisten them. The muscles around your eyes are also connected to the muscles around your heart via a system of arteries and nerves, so rubbing your eyes can also slow your heart rate, making you feel more relaxed and ready to sleep. But don't rub too hard: doing so can damage your lens or cornea. Much better to get to bed nice and early before the eye-rubbing even starts.

······················ **HERE'S THE RUB** ······················

❯ In 1960, Horlicks invented a condition called 'night starvation', and then advertised their own drink as the perfect solution.

❯ Even adults sleep better if gently rocked to sleep.

❯ A 2004 study found that people who slept on their right-hand side were less likely to have nightmares.

❯ Giant armadillos sleep for over 18 hours a day.

Where do all the birds go at night?

Contrary to cartoon depictions, most birds sleep in nests only when they are incubating their eggs or keeping their babies warm. The rest of the time, they tend to roost out of sight on roofs, ledges and in trees, picking places that will shelter them from the elements and predators.

You'd think birds would plummet to the ground as soon as they fall asleep, but they have a clever system in place to prevent this. They have 'flexor' tendons in their legs that automatically lock their toes around their chosen perch when they are ready to go to sleep. These pin the bird in place so that it stays upright naturally all night. The tendons relax when the bird wakes up.

Birds have been found sleeping in unexpected places, such as tin cans, old shoes and even the glove compartments of abandoned cars. And some of them can sleep while flying. Frigate birds, for instance, nap in 12-second chunks while airborne, which means they can stay on the wing for up to two months at a time.

What did a dinosaur's bottom look like?

. . . .

Dinosaurs are ancient relatives of reptiles and birds, so it was long assumed (by people who spend their time thinking about such things) that their bottoms were similar to those modern animals' rear ends. Snakes and sparrows both have a single hole for pooing and laying eggs. It's called a cloaca – which comes from the Latin word for 'sewer' – and scientists hypothesised that dinos probably had the same biological apparatus.

Then, in 2020, there was a breakthrough. A fossilised psittacosaurus (a relative of the triceratops) on display at the Museum of Natural History in Frankfurt was examined by a team of researchers, who discovered that the specimen was in such good condition that they could now answer this conundrum definitively: the posterior was covered in flaps of skin, which meant it was less like a chicken's rear end and more like a crocodile's. Snap!

In chess, why is the rook shaped like a castle and not like a bird?

Many chess grandmasters have made their pieces fly around the board, but the rook isn't named after the cousin of the crow. Its name comes from the Persian word *rukh*, meaning 'chariot', after the shape the piece took in an earlier version of the game called Shatranj. Nobody is quite sure how the chariot-shaped *rukh* morphed into the castle-like rook that we play with today.

In Bulgarian the piece is called 'the cannon', and in Russian it's 'the boat'. Bishops are also known by different names around the world: they're 'elephants' in Arabic, 'jesters' in French, 'camels' in Hindi and 'tortoises' in Georgian.

What is the point of the pawns?
Pawn strategy can be key to winning a game of chess. The pieces start out as the weakest on the board, but if manipulated correctly can be promoted to become extra queens.

In an older version of the game each pawn used to represent a different occupation: blacksmith, farmer, gambler, gatekeeper, innkeeper, merchant, physician and scribe.

Is it just me, or are parking spots too small?

. . . .

The real problem is that today's cars are too big.

The standard public parking space is exactly the same size as it was in the 1970s: 2.4 metres wide and 4.8 metres long. That's more than enough space for an older car, but today's runarounds are much larger. In 2018, the consumer group Which? found that more than 120 models on sale in the UK were too long to fit in a regular spot. Even standard-sized SUVs typically take up around 90% of a regulation parking space, which doesn't leave much room to open the doors.

Things got even harder for motorists in the town of Newbury in 2015, when over a hundred drivers were fined for parking outside the boundary lines of their bays. However, the spaces themselves were up to a metre shorter than they should have been. It took a retired architect with a measuring stick to point out the error.

If you're struggling to park, then maybe take a tip from the US, where 7% of people surveyed admitted that they have prayed to God to help them to find a good parking space. And if He isn't listening, you could always try St Frances Cabrini, the unofficial patron saint of car-parking. The Reverend Richard Coles has suggested those struggling to park could try saying the prayer 'Mother Cabrini, Mother Cabrini, please find a space for my parking machiney.'

If I lose weight, does Earth get lighter?

First of all, it's important to understand the difference between mass and weight. Mass is how much 'stuff' is inside something, and weight is a measure of the effect gravity has on that mass. If you go to the Moon, your body won't change, so your mass will stay the same. But your weight will be about one-sixth of what it is on Earth, because the Moon's gravity is only one-sixth as powerful as the Earth's. When we refer to losing or gaining *weight*, we actually mean *mass*.

Surprisingly, if you lose, say, 5 kg of mass, you breathe most of it out: 85% is converted to carbon dioxide; the rest is turned into water, which exits your body as tears, sweat and urine. This is because most fats are chains of molecules made from carbon, hydrogen and oxygen. As you breathe in fresh oxygen, it reacts with the fat; some of it attaches to the carbon to create carbon dioxide, and some attaches to the hydrogen and makes water. Since those 5 kilos still exist as carbon dioxide and water, when you get lighter, the Earth as a whole doesn't lose weight – or rather, it doesn't lose mass.

There are some gases that can leave the Earth and make it lighter. Unlike the relatively heavy carbon dioxide, hydrogen and helium – the two lightest elements in the universe – are both lighter than air, so can rise to the top of our atmosphere much more easily than, say, a piece of lead could. Once there, the atoms of gas can take in a rush of energy from the Sun's heat, which causes them to speed up and escape Earth's atmosphere. We lose 3 kg of hydrogen and helium every second, and 90,000 tonnes a year.

But the planet can also gain weight in the form of dust. Space is much dustier than you'd imagine (it is very old, after all). It's full of debris from the formation of the Solar System. Thanks to that, and the occasional meteorite, Earth gains about 45,000 tonnes a year.

Taking everything into account, Earth is getting slightly lighter – but don't panic! It weighs approximately 5,972,000,000,000,000,000,000 tonnes, and we're losing only about 0.000000000000001% of our mass annually. That's equivalent to you losing less than a single strand of hair from your head.

Why do my clothes turn inside out in the washing machine?

Disappointingly, there is limited research into this phenomenon. It's quite likely that the clothes get turned around between leaving your body and arriving in the machine. To be completely sure that it happens during the cycle, you'd need to check everything as it goes in and comes out. And that's exactly what a 14-year-old called Christie Conrad did in 1993. She focused on pants and found that over the course of a hundred washes, more than 50% of them flipped inside out. However, those with a wider waistband were more likely to stay the right way round, which suggests that further research is needed.

Christie's research took first place at the county science fair, and while she didn't win the competition at state level, an underwear company did get in touch to send the family more of the non-flipping kind, so in a way she still won.

Some early visitors to Yellowstone National Park cleaned their clothes by putting them into the geyser known as Old Faithful. One account from 1877 described how they bundled their garments into a pillowcase and threw it into the water; then, just as they began to fear their load was gone for good, the geyser erupted with a roar and the (now clean) clothes were 'mixed in every conceivable shape' as they shot 100 feet into the air, before landing back on the ground.

Astronauts on the International Space Station don't even bother with laundry. Their dirty clothes are loaded into a spacecraft, which then burns up in the Earth's atmosphere. To people on Earth, this will look like a dazzling meteor, so it's worth bearing in mind that next time you wish upon a shooting star, you might actually be wishing upon an astronaut's dirty socks.

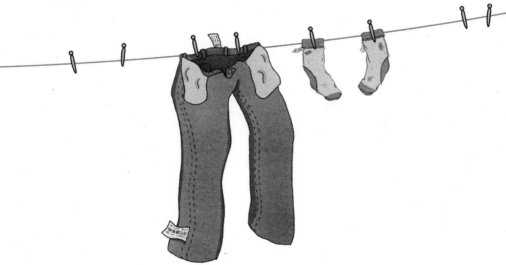

What's the point of dust jackets?

If your hardbacks are lined up neatly on a shelf, the dust jacket won't stop dust from settling on top of the pages. But it will protect the book's cover and spine from scratches and scrapes over the years.

Dust jackets used to work slightly differently from how they do today and would be wrapped around books, covering them entirely. They were then removed like wrapping paper when somebody wanted to read the contents. The oldest such jacket still in existence was discovered in the Bodleian Library's collection and dates back to 1830. It belonged to a book called *Friendship's Offering* and still had traces of sealing wax from the original wrappings.

Towards the end of the 19th century, publishers realised that dust jackets were the perfect place to add more information about a book, and so they evolved into the kind that covers this book (if you're reading the physical edition). It's worth hanging on to your dust jackets: missing ones can lower the price of a valuable book by 75–90%.

If you do have a beloved edition that is in particularly poor condition, you may want to visit Boston Public Library. They run a mini-carwash for freshening up books, though no water is involved. You put your tome on a conveyor belt, and it spins past brushes and moves through hanging plastic curtains to emerge refreshed. The machine can dust off 12 books per minute.

Who is the most successful novelist of all time?

Agatha Christie. She has sold a billion copies of her books in English and another billion in international editions, and is outsold by only Shakespeare (who was, of course, a playwright) and the Bible.

Born in Torquay in 1890, Christie began writing after her sister Madge bet her that she couldn't write a detective story. She went on to write 66 novels, 14 short stories and several works for theatre, including the world's longest-running play, *The Mousetrap*. During the First World War, she worked in a hospital pharmacy and developed such knowledge of poisons that one of her early books was mentioned in the *Pharmaceutical Journal*.

Christie once caused consternation at MI5 after she named a character 'Major Bletchley' in her novel *N or M?*, as they worried this meant she knew about the top-secret codebreaking efforts going on at Bletchley Park. She was friends with Bletchley codebreaker Dilly Knox, who asked her about the name. 'Bletchley?' replied Christie. 'My dear, I was stuck there on my way by train from Oxford to London and took revenge by giving the name to one of my least lovable characters.'

MI5 heaved a huge sigh of relief.

BAKER STREET

Did any sleuths actually work in Baker Street?

In fiction, 221B Baker Street is famously the address of Sherlock Holmes. In real life, it is now the home of the Sherlock Holmes Museum.

During the Second World War, the Special Operations Executive (SOE) – Britain's army of spies – was based at 64 Baker Street. In theory, it was a top-secret organisation, but despite the wartime campaign against loose lips sinking ships, bus conductors would shout, as they passed the SOE headquarters, that it was time for any spies to get off.

One of the many people who worked at no. 64 was Maud West (1880–1964), who spent a year there as a clerk during the war. Before this brief stint, she had had a longer career as a detective and was often referred to as 'Miss Sherlock Holmes' or 'London's Premier Lady Detective'. West ran her own detective agency and was famous for her use of disguises, with highlights including an elderly woman, a glamorous socialite and a fairly convincing Charlie Chaplin. On one occasion she managed to extract information by disguising herself as a fortune-teller, wearing a robe covered in moons and black cats, and tempting housemaids in a local servants' hall to reveal their secrets to her.

West wrote about her adventures for the newspapers, and her stream of anecdotes was endless, though some are thought to have been exaggerated in order to drum up publicity for her business. She recalled gaining access to a blackmailer's flat and drugging his coffee while she rescued incriminating letters belonging to her client. To prevent herself from being spotted while escaping, she slithered along the floor hidden underneath a tiger-skin rug. On another occasion, she was accosted in her office by a (different) blackmailer, who commented, 'I am fortunate in finding you alone, Miss West,' only for West to reply, 'Oh, not quite alone,' as she picked up a loaded revolver from her desk.

· · · · · · · · · · · · · · · YOU CAN'T HANDLE THE SLEUTH! · · · · · · · · · · · · · · ·

❯ MI5 initially employed Boy Scouts for information-gathering during the Second World War, but found they were unreliable and were inclined to brag about their work.

❯ During the First World War, Frieda Lawrence (wife of D. H.) was accused of being a spy and sending messages to German U-boats by hanging her red stockings in certain positions on her washing line.

❯ In the 20th century, many detectives suffered from mercury poisoning, as the powder used to dust for fingerprints was made by grinding up mercury and chalk.

Can you really crack a safe by listening to it with a stethoscope?

. . . .

In most cases, you absolutely can.

We spoke to David Kneafsey, a professional safe-cracker and member of the safe-crackers' professional body, the Safe and Vault Technicians Association. He has spent his career opening safes all over the world, from Hatton Garden to Hollywood, and told us that the principle of safe-cracking is so simple it can be taught in an hour, although in practice it takes a lifetime to master.

A standard safe lock consists of a set of interlocking wheels, and each wheel has a notch somewhere on it. To pull back the bolts on the door and open the safe, all three notches need to be lined up. You can't tell by sight which number will align each wheel correctly, but when a wheel reaches the right point and the notch lines up with the 'gate' inside, it makes a very tiny noise, and the stethoscope allows you to hear that sound. In the past, safe-crackers used a doctor's stethoscope, but modern stethoscopes are electronic and much more sensitive. Some are so powerful that if you place one at the top of a six-foot door and gently scratch the door's bottom, it will pick up that minute vibration. Some can even be tuned specifically to pick up the metal-on-metal sounds made by a safe's lock.

If the safe is still stumping you, then the next step is to use a drill to make a small hole near the lock, into which you insert a borescope – a device to help you see things you wouldn't normally spy with the naked eye – so you can see the notches on the wheels and line them up. Other techniques include using a robotic dialler, which automatically cycles through every possible combination, but that takes a while. Don't be tempted to use a sledgehammer on a safe: some of them have anti-theft technology that can detect brute force, causing them to seal themselves even tighter.

When the *New York Times* interviewed one of the world's best safe-crackers, Jeff Sitar, he revealed that he loves safe-cracking so much that he named his dog Combo. Some things still stump him, though: 'You should see the ribbing I get when I can't open a ketchup bottle,' he said.

Why do songs get stuck in my head?

These are commonly called 'earworms'. In a recent study, Journey's 'Don't Stop Believin'', Lady Gaga's 'Bad Romance' and, appropriately, Kylie Minogue's 'I Just Can't Get You Out of My Head' were noted as some of the tunes most likely to get stuck on repeat.

A 2011 survey carried out in Finland found that earworms affect around 90% of people at least once a week, so it's actually more unusual if you *don't* get the occasional song stuck in your head. It happens more often with songs that are upbeat and have more predictable elements. And songs are more likely to stay with you if you're feeling stressed. The idea is that if your brain already has a lot to process, it might grab hold of a repetitive idea – or tune – and stick with it.

Studies have suggested a few ways of dealing with earworms: chewing gum or trying to solve anagrams can help, as they give your brain another repetitive thing to think about. Or you could try a palate-cleanser song: 'Happy Birthday', 'God Save the Queen' and 'Karma Chameleon' have been found to be particularly effective at wiping stuck songs from your mind.

And if that palate-cleanser song gets stuck? Time to break out the anagrams . . .

Decipher the names of these Quite Interesting people:

Naive Salad

Oz Label

Vikings Toads*

* Turn to page 238 for the answers.

Why does my arm get pins and needles?

The scientific name for your limb going numb or tingling when you lean or lie on it at a weird angle for too long is 'paresthesia'. It is *not* caused by a lack of blood flow to the nerves, although sometimes it can feel like that.

The more likely culprit is nerve compression. You are simply squashing your nerves and making them malfunction. The constant stream of information those nerves send to your brain is temporarily disrupted, a bit like stepping on a garden hose. Some stop sending information completely (which is what makes the limb feel numb), and others fire erratic, nonsense information, which your brain interprets as pins and needles – the equivalent of static on a television not tuned to any channel.

The nerves nearly always recover quickly once the pressure is lifted and you've given your arm or leg a good shake. The rushing sensation that feels like blood returning to the extremities is a result of your nerves recovering.

If you are worried about your blood supply, paresthesia is only one of the symptoms. You can check for the other five 'p's: pain, pallor, pulselessness, paralysis and 'perishing' cold.

· **HARD FACT** ·

❯ Saturday-night palsy is a limp wrist that can last for several weeks, and is caused by sleeping on a hard chair with one arm over the back. It is so called because it most commonly happens to people who are the worse for wear after a big night out.

What are hiccups for, and why can't I get rid of them?

. . . .

During a hiccup, two bits of your body are pulling in different directions. Your arch-shaped diaphragm – the muscle under your lungs that pulls air in and out of them – suddenly clenches against your will. Usually, this would flatten it, causing the area above it to enlarge and suck air into the lungs. But during a hiccup, a flap in your windpipe called the epiglottis simultaneously snaps shut. Air is sucked in by the diaphragm, then abruptly blocked by the epiglottis, making a 'hic' sound in the process.

No one is sure why our bodies battle against themselves in such an irritating way, but scientists believe it's a leftover from 400 million years ago. This was when animals first began crawling out of water and learning to breathe on dry land. They evolved lungs so that they could breathe air, but they needed a way to make sure water didn't get into these new organs when they were in the water. The hiccup reflex may have been the answer; it sucked water across their gills so they could extract oxygen from it, but stopped it from entering their lungs and drowning them. Growing tadpoles require the same skills today, as they breathe both in and out of the pond. Studies show that their brains make the same patterns when they breathe as humans do when they hiccup, which does suggest that this theory holds water (sorry).

Another mystery is why humans and other mammals, such as cats and rats, have retained the ability to hiccup, but other animals, such as birds and lizards, have lost it. The explanation may lie in breastfeeding. Human foetuses begin to hiccup in the womb after just two months. This is useful muscular practice for when they emerge and need to suck milk from their mothers' breasts. In order to draw the liquid into their mouths they have to suck inwards but then quickly close their windpipes to keep the milk out of their lungs. Hiccupping prepares them perfectly for this action.

As for how to get rid of hiccups, scientists are still working on it. A five-year study into hiccups found that holding your breath, taking sips of water and holding your nose had only limited effect. The paper's author also commented that neither giving someone a fright nor drinking upside down were based on science.

It's not all bad news, though: in 2021, a team of researchers announced they'd designed a drinking straw that, when used, cured hiccups in 92% of volunteers. But this was a small study that has yet to be replicated, so for the time being, don't hold your breath.

· HICCUP THE PIECES ·

❯ The world record for the longest-ever bout of hiccups belongs to farmer Charles Osborne, who started hiccupping while carrying a 350 lb pig in 1894. The hiccups lasted 68 years, only disappearing a year before he died. Doctors believe it must have been caused by him bursting a blood vessel in his brain while lifting the hog.

How does a painkiller know where the pain is?

It doesn't.

When you touch something hot or stub your toe, the body begins its plan to heal itself and, crucially, ensure you don't do it again. It may not feel that way at the time, but pain is there to protect you. If, for example, you catch your hand on a kettle, the pain will encourage you to pull away to avoid a more severe burn.

From the moment an injury occurs, chemicals are created and released at the site of the incident. These then stimulate the nervous system, which sends signals to your brain. The brain interprets these as pain, but it also tells your body to send more blood to the area. This is why an injury often becomes red and swollen.

If you take some paracetamol or ibuprofen for the pain, the pill will dissolve in your stomach, and the medicine will travel around in your bloodstream, visiting all parts of your body. The painkiller stops the injured cells from making and releasing the pain-causing chemicals, and as a result, the messages can't reach your brain. This means that not only do you feel less pain, the inflammation or swelling is also lessened. But be warned: medication can cause side effects, and ironically one of the potential side effects of ibuprofen is headaches.

Why do snakes shed their skin?

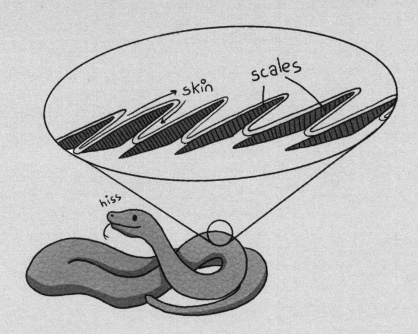

A snake's skin doesn't grow with its body like ours does, so it has to get rid of it when it gets too small or worn out. The scientific name for skin-shedding is ecdysis, and many animals do it, including humans. We shed millions of tiny individual flakes every day, but snakes do it all in one go.

Shedding usually begins with the skin around the eyes and mouth, which becomes saggy. Instead of eyelids, snakes have transparent eye caps that cover the eyes completely, and these turn foggy, making it difficult to see. To get it out of the way, the snake instinctively rubs its head against something hard, like a rock or the ground. From that point, the skin begins to break up and naturally peels off as the snake slides around. It's like wearing big socks and sliding backwards along a carpet – eventually friction will pull them off. Depending on the snake, the process can take anywhere from a few hours to a couple of weeks.

Even though it looks like it is wrapped flat around the snake, the skin actually covers both sides of every scale, so it's continuously folded back on itself, like an unpleasant Viennetta. When shed and stretched out flat, it can be twice as long as the snake itself.

························ **A SLITHER OF TRUTH** ·······················

❯ Arizona rattlesnakes cuddle with their friends.

❯ Hours after being decapitated, snakes retain their reflexes and can give you a deadly bite.

❯ In 2020, following an incident on a bus, Transport for Greater Manchester stated that live snakes are not acceptable Covid face coverings.

Can I hatch an egg that I bought from the supermarket?

Probably not. That said, in 2019, 14-year-old William Atkins hatched a Waitrose duck egg using a £40 incubator that he bought on eBay. The healthy duckling was called Jeremy and was, at the insistence of William's mother, donated to a local farm.

In theory, nothing should happen when a shop-bought egg is put in an incubator, which makes Jeremy something of a miracle. In order for an egg to hatch it needs to be fertilised, and most farms that provide eggs to major retailers keep their female birds separated from any males to ensure there's no chance of that happening. In this instance, the egg producer said its ducks had outdoor access, where they may have met a wild drake.

If a fertilised egg does wind up in a supermarket, then without some form of incubation – either a mother sitting on it or an electronic incubator – the embryo won't begin to grow, so you wouldn't be able to notice the difference.

We get hen's eggs, duck eggs and goose eggs, so why do we never see turkey eggs in the supermarket?

Chickens are much more efficient egg-layers. Each one produces around 300 eggs per year, against a turkey's average of 110. Turkeys also become more aggressive than chickens if you try to remove their eggs, so most of them are kept for breeding and for the festive period, when we eat between 7 and 8 million birds. If you want to try a turkey egg, you might have more luck at a farmers' market.

Why are we told to keep eggs in the fridge, but supermarkets have them on a shelf?
The British Egg Industry Council, which is responsible for the 'Lion Mark' on eggs that meet its stringent standards, says that eggs should be stored at temperatures below 20°C. Supermarkets are usually kept cooler than this, so they can keep their eggs safely on shelves, but as the temperature of private homes can vary, the best place for your eggs is in the fridge.

How do baby birds breathe inside their eggs?

Eggshells look solid, but they actually contain thousands of tiny pores that let oxygen in for the developing chick and also let carbon dioxide out.

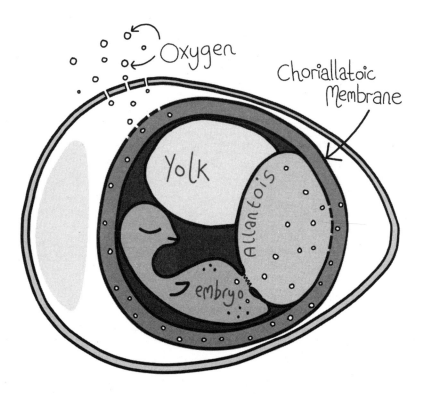

Baby birds don't breathe with their lungs until just before they hatch, so there is an extra mechanism for them to get oxygen. The chick has a pouch of membranes called the allantois (which means 'sausage-shaped'), which is the equivalent of a human placenta. One end plugs into the chick's gut, while the other is positioned near the inner surface of the eggshell and connects to another network of blood vessels called the chorioallantoic membrane, which is spread across the egg's interior.

Once the oxygen gets through the eggshell, it passes into the chorioallantoic membrane, then into the blood, and eventually into the chick's body. Carbon dioxide moves the other way. The chick also gets rid of other waste as it develops – this all passes into the allantois and is left behind as the chick hatches. The mechanism is effectively an exterior lung and digestive system all in one.

The egg gradually loses moisture as the chick develops, and space builds up, forming a growing air pocket inside the egg. Shortly before it hatches, the chick starts breathing from that air pocket, giving it the strength to get out. The air pocket also lets the baby bird chirp inside the egg, telling its parents and its clutch-mates that it's about to hatch.

· SHELL SHOCKER ·

❯ Baby birds' necks contain a musculus complexus, also known as the 'hatching muscle', which helps them crack their way out of the egg.

If our normal body temperature is 37°C, then why do we feel too hot when the temperature outside is only in the 20s?

It's true that the average core body temperature for humans is around 37°C, but that isn't the whole story. You are constantly radiating heat. All the work your body does to keep you alive – pumping blood, moving your limbs, keeping every cell going – generates a great deal of heat energy. To lose heat we exhale warm breath, pump blood to the surface of our skin and sweat.

Heat naturally seeks a state of equilibrium, where everything meets at a similar point, which is why cups of tea go cold and icy drinks end up lukewarm if left out long enough, both drinks eventually becoming the temperature of the surrounding air. Your body is the same. Although your core temperature measures in the high 30s, these processes to get rid of your body's heat work best when the outside temperature is about 21°C. If it is very warm, your body will find it much harder to push that heat out.

This effect is even stronger when the air around you is humid. Our bodies are very good at removing heat via beads of sweat, which carry lots of heat to the surface of our skin and then evaporate away, leaving us cooler. If the air is already very damp or there's no breeze, then the sweat can't evaporate, meaning you will feel especially hot and uncomfortable. So, just like in real life, the further you get from 21, the harder it is to feel cool.

Thermal leggings are called 'long johns'. So who was John?

It's commonly believed that long johns are named after John L. Sullivan, a 19th-century boxer who admittedly did wear tights in the ring that look a bit like the modern underwear. But the evidence is not cast-iron.

Sullivan, also known as the 'Boston Strong Boy', once toured the US, offering $1,000 (around $27,000 today) to anyone who could last 12 minutes in the ring against him. Nobody did. He died in 1918, and the first known reference to 'long johns', meaning 'long underwear', came 23 years later, in 1941, when an army recruit wrote home explaining he'd been issued with long johns. Sullivan was still well known then, so it is possible they were named after him, and in 1944 a newspaper explicitly made that claim. But during his lifetime the only reference to him as 'Long John' was made in a newspaper in 1893, and that's about it.

The phrase 'Long John' pre-dated Sullivan himself, which is further evidence against the theory. In the early 1800s, it was a slang term for a tall person – possibly a corrupted version of the French phrase *longues jambes*, meaning 'long legs'. 'Long John' was also a nickname for two species of South American tree, the *Triplaris americana* and the *Triplaris weigeltiana*; their branches start very high up their trunks, so they resemble a tall person. And, from 1905, a 'Long John' was a type of long, iced doughnut.

The longest Johns were John Rogan and John Carroll, the second- and third-tallest people who ever lived. Unfortunately, we don't know anything about their choice of thermals.

Why does 'inflammable' mean 'flammable'?

'Inflammable' came first. The *Oxford English Dictionary* records its first usage in 1605, but the related word 'inflame' is even older.

Due to confusion about the 'in-' potentially meaning 'not' – as seen in words like 'inactive' or 'ineffective' – the word 'flammable' (first used in the early 1800s) is now often preferred. The confusion actually dates back even further, as 'inflammable' and 'flammable' come from different Latin words – *inflammare* and *flammare* respectively – which had subtly different meanings. The first meant 'to do an action and cause something to be set on fire', while the second meant something more like 'to become alight'.

The opposite of both versions is 'non-flammable', which means something is unlikely to catch fire.

How do stinging nettles sting?

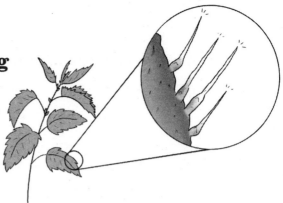

Nettle leaves are covered with tiny hollow hairs, which break off when touched and act like hypodermic needles, injecting a cocktail of chemicals into your skin. Scientists are still trying to isolate all the ingredients of this cocktail, but we know the main culprit is histamine, which is also found in wasp and bee stings.

Histamine is always in your body, and it's important. If a foreign invader, such as a splinter or a virus, gets under your skin, then histamine is released, which opens the blood vessels and allows your body's defences to flood the area. However, nettles and stinging insects use that protection against us. They inject *too much* histamine into your body, which causes swelling and pain as your body tries to remove an invader that doesn't necessarily exist. From the wasp's or nettle's point of view, if it can cause enough discomfort, then you might leave it alone in the future.

In Britain, it's traditional to apply a dock leaf to a nettle sting, but there's no known reason why that would help. It's often said that dock sap is alkaline and counters the acid of the sting – but in fact it isn't. Others say that dock contains a natural antihistamine, but there's no evidence that this is true either. It's probably just the placebo effect, or that the distraction of looking for dock leaves takes your mind off the nettle sting.

Is it true that inside every fig there is a dead wasp?

There may have been a dead wasp or two in your fig, but they should hopefully be long gone.

Today, most commercial fig growers do not use wasps, but in the wild it's a different tale. The Agaonidae family – known as 'fig wasps' – pollinate fig trees, and have done for millions of years. In exchange, the figs provide somewhere for the wasps to hatch their eggs safely.

Although fig trees don't appear to have any flowers, the fruit of a fig is actually lots of tiny flowers inside a fleshy stem. When you eat one, you'll notice lots of little crunchy bits. These are the seeds, and each seed is inside a flower.

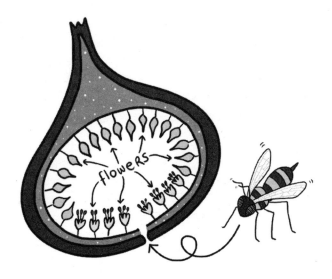

When the flowers are ready to be pollinated, they send out an aroma that attracts pregnant female fig wasps. The wasp crawls inside through a hole at the base of the fig, which is so narrow that she loses her wings and antennae in the process. She also carries the pollen from the fig where she was born, and once inside uses it to pollinate the fig flowers. She then lays her eggs, ensuring the survival of her children, before she dies inside the fig.

The eggs develop into larvae and then into wasps. When they emerge, the male wasps mate with the females, who then fly away, taking their fig's pollen with them, ready to pollinate the next fig. The male wasps don't have wings, so, like their mother, they also die inside the fig.

You would expect figs to contain lots of dead wasps, but the fig produces an enzyme that completely digests the corpses. So tuck in.

. . . . **GENERAL FIGNORANCE** . . . .

❯ Fig trees were on Earth before the dinosaurs became extinct.

❯ Figs are probably the oldest domesticated crop. They were plucked from trees in Jericho over 11,000 years ago.

❯ People in Uganda produce cloth from the bark of fig trees.

❯ St Fiacre is the patron saint of haemorrhoids. During the Middle Ages, piles were known as 'St Fiacre's figs'.

How deep do you have to bury a body?

If conditions are right, you can be just two feet under.

In the UK, the Ministry of Justice's guidelines on natural burials specify that in a normal municipal cemetery, the top of a coffin has to be a minimum of three feet from the top of the soil. But if you're being buried in a perishable coffin, you can be even shallower – as little as two feet from ground level. In most US states, it's even less: you need just 18 inches of soil between the top of the body and the surface to ensure that no smells escape and the body is safe from scavenging animals.

There's a chance you'll end up deeper than six feet under as some cemeteries stack up to three bodies in a single grave. A double grave needs to be seven feet deep and a triple needs to be nine.

The 'six feet under' idea dates back to at least 1665. The rules during that year's Great Plague specified that 'all the graves shall be at least six foot deep'. They also recommended that hackney coachmen – aka cabbies – should leave their cabs empty for six days after taking infected people to the 'pest-house'. Other rules included 'no hogs to be allowed to stray in the streets', as well as the banning of plays, games and the singing of ballads.

In 2017, a company called Sacred Stones, who make pagan-style burial mounds where urns can be interred, won the 'What to Do with the Ashes' award at the Good Funeral Awards (aka the 'Death Oscars'). There are also companies who can turn your ashes into diamonds, incorporate them into fireworks or even send them into space.

What's the sweetest way to go?

In 1597, Chinese naturalist Li Shih-chen published *Chinese Materia Medica*, a compendium of all the plants, animals and procedures known to Chinese medicine at the time. In it he described a process called 'mellification'.

Supposedly practised in Arabia, elderly male volunteers would eat nothing but honey. They would also bathe in it, and after a month would start sweating and defecating honey. Once death finally took them, they would be sealed in a honey-filled coffin for 100 years. After the allotted time, the container was opened and the resulting substance used to treat broken bones and ingested as a cure-all. Li Shih-chen does say that he heard of this practice second-hand, and so cannot completely testify to its authenticity.

The preservative powers of honey have been well recognised throughout history, and it was used to embalm the dead in many different cultures. Herodotus wrote that ancient Assyrians did this, and Alexander the Great is said to have been buried in a golden casket filled with honey. It was rumoured that the first four earls of Southampton were also buried this way, and when workmen were asked to deal with subsidence in the vault in the early 1900s, one of them supposedly noticed liquid oozing from a coffin. He ran his finger across it and confirmed that it was indeed honey.

Ancient Egyptians, Assyrians, Chinese, Greeks and Romans all used honey in the treatment of wounds or diseases. Modern studies have revealed that it does have some antibacterial properties and can inhibit the growth of yeast, fungi and some viruses – but we'd always advise seeking a doctor's advice before reaching for the honey.

Why do we crave sugar?

· ·

Because once upon a time that was a very good idea.

If you look back across the millions of years of evolutionary history, humans have had reliable access to food from agriculture and industry for only a tiny fraction of that timeline. For the majority of our existence, we have fed ourselves through the far less reliable methods of hunting and gathering.

Back then, you were only likely to come across sugar in its natural form – fruit. Fruit was harder to come by than other food sources (such as vegetables and nuts) due to its seasonal nature and short window of ripeness. The natural sugars provided plenty of energy, so if you found a stash of fresh fruit, it made evolutionary sense to eat as much of it as possible, because you might not see it again for weeks or even months.

Sugar also helps your body to store fat. Humans who sought it out were more likely to have reliable fat reserves for the times when food was unavailable and therefore survived for longer. Since seeking out and eating sugar could help prevent starvation, our brains and bodies evolved to release mood-enhancing chemicals when we consume it, creating the cravings.

Fast-forward to the present day, and we still have those same genes that make us crave sugary food, even when we are not at risk of starvation. We are also no longer limited by the seasons or the need to climb a tall fruit tree to get our sugar kick. We can simply treat ourselves to a Snickers bar.*

* Other brands of chocolate are available.

Is it true that the average person swallows eight spiders a year while they're asleep?

Absolutely not.

In 1993, technology journalist Lisa Holst wrote an article in *PC Professional* examining the claim that people will believe anything they read online. She made up her own ridiculous 'facts', similar to those found on the early Internet, and the 'eight spiders a year' statistic was one of her outlandish inventions. To perfectly prove Holst's point, it then got circulated as a real fact, when actually it's a web of deceit.

Why are people so terrified of spiders?

There are contradictory schools of thought on this one.

A study by the Emory University School of Medicine found that fear can be passed on through our DNA, and a 2015 Cornell University study suggested that this could be the case for the fear of spiders. In their experiment 252 people were asked to watch a computer screen filled with abstract shapes. When a distorted image of a spider appeared, participants recognised it far faster than they did a clearer image of a fly or a needle. The team described this as 'reflexive awareness'. For millions of years, humans were more likely to encounter dangerous spiders than we are today, so it could be an evolutionary mechanism that prompts us to react quickly if we see one.

There is still some debate over whether a fear of spiders is instinctive or learnt – and one of the best ways to test this is by experimenting on babies, as they are yet to develop socially learnt reactions.

In 2017, a team of German researchers showed images of spiders and flowers to six-month-old babies while they sat on the laps of their parents, who were wearing opaque sunglasses so they couldn't see the images and subconsciously influence their children's reactions. As the babies looked at the pictures, the size of their pupils was tracked.

The team found that the babies' pupils were significantly bigger when looking at a spider rather than a flower, even if the two were the same size and colour. This indicated that their brains' noradrenergic system, which processes stress, was more active. Similar results were achieved when images of snakes and fish were shown.

However, not all researchers agree that a fear of snakes and spiders is ingrained: a study of seven-month-olds found that they recognised snakes more quickly than other objects but showed no particular fear.

If you are someone who is scared of spiders, help is on the way. There is ongoing work to devise the steps you could take to conquer your fear. Research has shown that wearing a virtual reality headset and watching a CGI spider crawl over your hand can help. While it might sound like a nightmare, this safe, controlled exposure is a common technique used in tackling phobias. It has even been shown that watching scenes from a Spider-Man film featuring spiders makes people more comfortable around the real thing.

If you don't have access to a VR headset or you aren't a fan of the Marvel Universe, there is another technique: clinical hypnotherapist Adam Cox gets his patients to draw brightly coloured spiders with big eyes and smiley faces, thus enabling them to create positive associations with our eight-legged friends.

· · · · · · · · · · · · · · · · · · · WIDER SPIDER FACTS ·

❯ Spiders seem bigger the more scared you are.

❯ Most spiders are scared of ants.

❯ The Australian Broadcasting Corporation deemed an episode of *Peppa Pig* unsuitable for broadcast because its theme was 'spiders are very small and they can't hurt you'.

Spiders build webs to catch prey, but why don't they get caught in their own webs?

Spiders have several methods to prevent themselves from being caught by their own web. First, they can make both sticky and non-sticky sections. Orb-weaving spiders, for example, build their webs using scaffold-like threads that shoot out from the centre like the spokes of a wheel. These are non-sticky, unlike the threads which spiral around them.

While spinning a web, spiders can't always avoid touching the sticky parts, but they don't get stuck because only a small part of their bodies comes into contact with them. A spider's legs are covered in tiny hair-like structures called setae, and it is these that touch the sticky web.

On the other hand, when a fly hits the web, a large amount of its body touches it at once, which means the fly is more likely to get stuck and become the spider's supper.

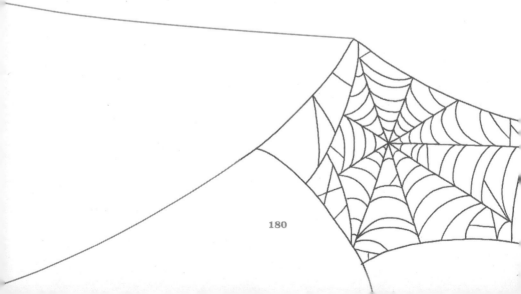

Can an aeroplane fly through a rainbow?

If you fly a plane towards a rainbow, the rainbow will move away from you at the same speed and you'll never catch up with it.

Rainbows are an optical illusion that appear when sunlight strikes raindrops at a very precise angle, causing it to split into many different wavelengths and colours, which then travel to our eyes. If you change position, you will see a different rainbow to the one you were originally looking at. This also means that while two people can see a rainbow at the same time, it will look slightly different to both of them, even if they are standing side by side.

What you can do is fly through someone else's rainbow. If you were on the ground looking up, then you might see an aeroplane fly through one, but the people on the plane wouldn't know as they would be seeing a different rainbow altogether.

If you're lucky and see a rainbow from the window of a plane, you might notice that it's actually a circle. Most of the rainbows we see from the ground appear to be semicircles because we aren't high enough to see the whole thing.

The longest-lasting rainbow ever was spotted in Taiwan in 2017. It stayed in the sky for 8 hours and 58 minutes – about as long as a flight from London to Mumbai.

························· A DASH OF COLOUR ······················

❯ So-called 'white rainbows' appear when the water droplets in the air are too fine to refract light into different colours. These are also known as 'fogbows'.

Are we the only ones who like making sandcastles?

We're not. There are some keen builders in the animal world too.

Perhaps the most impressive is the sandcastle worm (technically known as *Phragmatopoma californica*) found off the west coast of America. Thousands of them club together to make structures that can be several metres long. They are less like our sandcastles and more like honeycombs, with one worm creating and living in each hole, and the whole structure is strong enough to survive the beating of the tides. Each worm makes its tube by gathering debris (like sand grains and bits of shell), using the tentacles on its head, and then secreting a sort of sticky cement that binds the material onto the cylinder that surrounds it. Even more impressively, the worms glue their castles together underwater.

Lake Malawi, in East Africa, contains around 200 different species of fish called cichlids, which build underwater sand structures, or 'bowers', in the hope of attracting a mate. The bowers can measure up to 10 feet across – 30 times larger than a male cichlid himself – and the fish build them by picking up sand in their mouths and painstakingly dropping it into place. If the sandcastle is impressive enough, a female fish will lay her eggs in the centre. Once the eggs have been fertilised, she then keeps them in her mouth, meaning she can't eat until they hatch a few weeks later.

The sand martin bird builds sand dungeons, rather than sandcastles. The males burrow half a metre into a sandbank with their claws and then sing outside the entrance in the hope

of attracting a mate to lay eggs inside the chamber. In 2021, professional human sand sculptors built a 400-tonne sand structure at a nature reserve in Surrey in order to encourage sand martins to nest there. The hope is that the birds will move in and adapt it, thus making it one of the world's first sandcastles built by two species in collaboration.

Why are we not allowed to smile in passport photos?

This has been the rule in the UK since 2004. The official advice is that you must 'have a plain expression and your mouth closed'. This is because facial recognition software is more effective when people have their mouths closed.

In 2016, a French civil servant went to court, asking that people be allowed to smile in their photos to give the country a morale boost. He argued that perhaps a closed-mouth smile, like the *Mona Lisa*'s, could be allowed, hoping that happier passport photos might cheer people up and also give the rest of the world a positive impression of France. The court ruled to keep the no-smiling rule.

Britain's first passports were handed out during the reign of Henry V, who ruled from 1413 until 1422, and they allowed the bearer to pass through certain foreign cities safely and without paying fees.

One of the oldest surviving passports was issued on 18 June 1641 and was signed personally by Charles I. By the early 1900s, British passports included a photo, a signature and a description, including 'shape of face' and 'features'. A similar change had occurred in America in the 1800s, when almost everyone described their features as 'average'.

Why do film-makers use green screens?

....

Green screens are used to create virtual backgrounds and special effects, but they weren't always green. The first-ever 'green screen' was actually black. In the 1900s, pioneering French film-maker Georges Méliès discovered that if you filmed a scene but left part of the picture completely black, then that area of the film reel would be left unexposed and unused. So if you rewound and filmed again with the same reel, this time putting an actor in that previously black space, the two takes would be merged into one.

In the 1960s, film-makers began to use a 'yellow-screen' technique: actors were filmed in front of a screen lit by sodium-vapour lamps that gave off the same warm yellow light as you got from old street lamps. This light has a very specific frequency, which meant a camera could be built with a prism inside that separated the sodium-coloured light from the other colours. The result was two film reels containing the same scene: one with just the actors and no background, and the other with just the background but no actors (and instead actor-shaped holes). If you replaced the background film with an all-new scene and then put them both together again, they would fit perfectly like a jigsaw puzzle, creating an incredibly crisp, clean, realistic special effect.

Walt Disney used this technique in the 1960s to film the scenes in *Mary Poppins* where the live-action actors interact with an animated world. The effect was so precise that even the delicate decorative lace veil on Mary Poppins's hat was perfectly removed from its background and transplanted into a cartoonscape. It was an Oscar-winning effect; the only problem was that the prism camera was extremely fiddly and difficult to calibrate. In fact, only one was ever successfully built and used by Hollywood.

The proper name for modern green-screening is 'keying', and rather than using analogue film, it is a digital computer process that takes an image and removes all the bits that are a certain 'key' colour. In theory, this key can be set to any colour, but it works most effectively if it is different from that of the people and objects you're filming. Bright green or blue are used most often, partly because they're easy to light and modern digital cameras can 'see' them better, and partly because they are unlikely to match your actors' clothes or hair.

It isn't a totally foolproof method, of course. The 2002 *Spider-Man* movie suffered production headaches when the red-and-blue-suited Spider-Man shared screen time with his nemesis, the Green Goblin, who gets his name from the colour of his costume.

Lit with Sodium Vapour Light

Lit with normal light

all other colours → ← sodium vapour light

Prism

Actor isolated on unexposed film

Background isolated around unexposed cut-out of actor.

Why do we produce tears when we are upset?

There are three kinds of tears: basal, which lubricate your eyes; reflex, which are produced when an irritant such as dust gets in your eye; and psychic, which are emotional tears.

Nobody really knows why we produce emotional tears. In the 1600s, there was a theory that emotions such as love literally warmed your heart, which then produced steam to cool down, and this would be released as tears from your eyes.

A more plausible modern theory is that crying encourages bonding, so we cry when we're overwhelmed or sad in order that others can pick up on these signals and provide support.

What about crocodile tears?

In humans, these are fake, insincere tears. The expression was popularised when a book published in the 1400s reported that crocodiles had been seen 'slaying men then eating them, weeping'. Crocs do actually cry when they eat, but probably not out of remorse. One possible explanation is that because they emerge from the water to eat, their eyes will dry out if not kept lubricated. Another theory is that their eyes are already wet from the water. Or it could be because they hiss and huff while eating, which generates air that passes through their sinuses and causes the tears.

Why do teeth need nerves?

For two key reasons: sensation and protection.

'Proprioception' is the sense of knowing where your body parts are. This is important with your arms and legs when walking and your fingers when typing, but it is equally important when it comes to your teeth. The nerves send a signal to your brain, letting it know where your teeth are in relation to a chunk of food, so that you can make tiny adjustments to the way you bite and chew.

The nerves in your teeth are also sensitive to temperature, acidity and sweetness. If you get tooth pain when eating, that's a warning sign that a trip to the dentist may be in order, to check for damage or decay to the enamel which usually protects your nerves. These nerves can also let you know if something is stuck in your teeth, which is especially useful before a video conference call.

Why do I get brain freeze when I eat ice cream?
When you take a mouthful of ice cream, it makes the back of your throat colder. This is where you find both the internal carotid artery (which sends blood to the brain) and the anterior cerebral artery (which is where your brain tissue starts). The cold causes these two blood vessels to contract and dilate, and receptors called the meninges between the two arteries pick this movement up and send signals to your brain. Your brain interprets these signals as pain, resulting in brain freeze – or sphenopalatine ganglioneuralgia, to give it its technical name.

What is the hardest tongue-twister in the world?

You may have grown up practising 'She sells seashells on the seashore', but there are some even more fiendish ones out there.

The *Guinness Book of World Records* used to list 'The sixth sick sheik's sixth sheep's sick' as the hardest in the English language, although Guinness don't keep track of this record any more. Globally, they noted a Xhosa tongue-twister as the most difficult one in the world. It goes, '*Iqaqa laziqikaqika kwazw kwaqhawaka uqhoqhoqha*,' which means, 'The skunk rolled down and ruptured its larynx.' In Xhosa, the last word contains three clicks.

In 2013, a team at the Massachusetts Institute of Technology who were researching tongue-twisters found one that proved so difficult that participants in their study would just give up. The fiendish phrase? 'Pad kid poured curd pulled cod.'

If you can say any of those quickly 10 times, award yourself five *QI* points.

· FINAL TWIST ·

❯ Inspired by mercenaries who were attempting a coup in the Seychelles in 1981, a journalist made up this tongue-twister: 'They shell seashores in the Seychelles.'

QI Tongue-Twisters

*Two blue whales wailed 'boo' in Wales
while truly blue.*

*When I queue quietly, QI quips
quite quickly and quite quaintly but
constantly quite interestingly.*

*12 elves place their books on shelves,
then two elves take themselves a book.
If 10 more elves write books themselves,
then how many books on elves'
bookshelves?*

*An aye-aye watched QI and sighed,
'Aye, my IQ is high, so why
Am I so shy and won't apply
To be an aye-aye on QI?'*

Where is last Wednesday?

It's still there, some say.

This was a question asked by the late, great actor, writer, director and mentor Ken Campbell (1941–2008), and it's a question about time. Everybody knows what time is, but try to describe it and your mind turns to slurry. Scientists disagree as to whether it even exists. A lot of the big equations in physics work better without it, Einstein called it 'a stubbornly persistent illusion', and philosophers have been arguing about the nature of time for at least 2,500 years.

Presentism, first proposed by the ancient Greek philosopher Heraclitus, is the theory that only the present is real and neither past nor future exist. At the other extreme is eternalism, the brainwave of Heraclitus' younger contemporary, Parmenides, which holds that past, present and future are all equally real. Occupying the middle ground is possibilism, the theory that past and present are both real, but there's no such thing as the future, and there never will be. Has your mind turned to slurry yet?

Eternalism got a shot in the arm from science in 1908, when Polish-born mathematician Hermann Minkowski, who had taught Einstein, took a hard look at his former pupil's special theory of relativity, published three years earlier in 1905. To considerable alarm, he announced that it implied space and time are one and the same thing, which exists permanently in a four-dimensional model called 'the block universe'.

One way of thinking about this is to compare time to a landscape. When you leave your house and walk down the road, it doesn't disappear when you go round the corner. New York is still there when you jump on a flight home. In the same way, as the present moves on (with you in it), the past is still sitting there behind you. It's not going anywhere. Many scientists who can't bring themselves to believe in a deity or an afterlife find this comforting because it means that if somebody they love dies in the present, they're still alive and well – and real – in the past.

One dispiriting drawback of eternalism is that the future is already mapped out and can't be changed, meaning you have absolutely zero free will. Hence possibilism, which is also known as growing-block time or the growing-block universe. According to this theory, the past – including last Wednesday – still exists, but as the present moves on, its leading edge rolls like a wave up an empty beach into the non-existent nothingness we call the future, leaving the solid past in its wake.

So there is no future. Not even a next Wednesday.

On the other hand, last Wednesday never dies.

Sounds like a Bond movie . . .

'Have you been involved in an accident that wasn't your fault?'

Since the 1800s, salespeople have been reading their scripts to non-consenting phone owners in the hope that they might make a quick buck. By 1879, it was such a common occurrence in America that a whistle-blower called Bates Harrington wrote a book called *How 'Tis Done*, which had the snappy subtitle *A Thorough Ventilation of the Numerous Schemes Conducted by Wandering Canvassers, Together with the Various Advertising Dodges for the Swindling of the Public*. In the book he explained the various tricks that people employed to sell atlases, insurance and even lightning rods.

It's essentially a numbers game. In 2011, researchers in Texas made more than 6,000 cold calls concerning real estate and found that they got one appointment or referral for every 209 calls they made. Those calls represented 7.5 hours of work, so if a company sells a product with a high enough value and pays its callers a low enough salary, it does make financial sense.

Does anyone like getting calls from unknown numbers?

A 2021 study found that Maasai men in Tanzania are very likely to strike up a conversation if called by someone they don't know. The Maasai look after animals over large areas and don't come across many other people in their day-to-day life, but social contacts are still very important for future business. So if they get a call from someone who also speaks the Maa language, they're unlikely to hang up. In fact, 46% of Maasai men have become friends with someone who got the wrong number and mistakenly called their phone.

Why are Turner's paintings so hazy?

J. M. W. Turner's unique aesthetic is often attributed to his depressive disposition, and in older age his deteriorating eyesight, which was exacerbated by the practice of looking directly into the Sun. At the time, doing so was thought to rest and recharge the eyes, but now we know it can be very damaging.

According to Christos Zerefos, Greece's leading climate-change scientist, the muddy skies in paintings like Turner's 1828 *Chichester Canal* were inspired by actual skies. When volcanic pollution – a mixture of ash and gas – is in the air, sunsets can seem much more colourful, so Zerefos looked at 124 high-quality images from the Tate Gallery in London, including many works by Turner, and found that in the 'volcanic' years – years with large eruptions and the three that followed them – the paintings had more red in their sunsets.

For example, in 1815, Mount Tambora in the Dutch East Indies erupted, and for the next 12 months debris spread across the globe, effectively frosting up the atmosphere with dust and gas. Average temperatures dropped by several degrees and the result was frightening, unusual weather. It became known as 'The Year Without a Summer' and had a disastrous impact on agriculture.

Turner's paintings are fading over time; it's as if the weather in each one is still changing. He prioritised materials such as carmine (a red pigment extracted from certain insects), choosing those that looked best when freshly applied – despite knowing that they wouldn't last long on canvas.

Other techniques he used to improve his artworks included wiping tobacco juice and stale beer on them, and spitting on the canvas.

The ash clouds that inspired Turner coincided with a second phenomenon that darkened the skies. In 1816, strange dark spots – sometimes described as 'black bile' – appeared on the surface of the Sun. They were big enough to be seen without a telescope, and an astronomer in Bologna claimed that these spots signalled the impending death of the Sun, which he said would happen on 18 July 1816. (In fact, they were harmless sunspots – cooler, darker patches on the Sun's surface.)

As the fateful day approached, riots broke out across Europe. Austria had to use its military forces to maintain public order, and the French government launched a public information campaign to educate the country's population about the harmlessness of sunspots. The day passed, the Sun continued to shine, and the unnatural conditions eventually passed. But we can see its effect on the world's psyche today: 1816 was the year that Lord Byron, his physician John Polidori and Mary Shelley hunkered down at the Villa Diodati with their friends to wait out the stormy weather, writing ghost stories by candlelight and giving the world both *The Vampyre* and *Frankenstein*.

How can I get my own blue plaque on my house?

It's complicated.

The London blue plaques scheme awards a dozen new memorial plates each year, and there are strict eligibility criteria. First, you have to die. Then wait 20 years. Then hope that someone nominates you. Then keep your fingers crossed that a panel of experts thinks yours is a worthy nomination – and in the top 12 received that year. Even if the panel says yes, you still have to hope that they are able to get permission from the owner of the house in which you lived: some people like having the plaque displayed, while others don't want to give tourists an excuse to stand outside their home taking photos.

Being male helps – less than 20% of the plaques in London are for women – as does being white – less than 5% celebrate people of colour. English Heritage says it is working to redress these imbalances.

Alternative schemes are run by councils and organisations across the country, so you could try a group with less stringent criteria; failing that, you could simply buy your own blue plaque and place it on the front of your house. English Heritage, who look after the official scheme, can't stop you unless you copy their design. To a blue-plaque spotter, the telltale sign that a plaque is official is that it doesn't have screws – English Heritage plaques are always embedded into the brickwork.

The content is also sometimes a clue: fans of Monty Python's Graham Chapman, annoyed that he was not given an official plaque on the 20th anniversary of his death in 2009, erected one in his memory, which reads: 'Jacob von Hogflume, 1864–1909, inventor of time travel, lived here in 2189'.

Where did surnames come from?

Before 1066, people in England were like Cher or Madonna – everyone knew them by a single name. That worked well when communities were small, but as towns grew bigger, an extra title was needed to distinguish between people who had the same name. A town might be home to Laura the Wise, James the Handsome or Anne the Miller. That name was used only by that person – it wasn't passed down to their children.

Surnames that are handed down through the generations came with the Norman Conquest. They were associated with land ownership, so the son of William of Calais might be called Henry of Calais. The English began to copy the practice, starting with the landowners; people who didn't own land continued to use the extra name they were known by. By the end of the 14th century, almost everyone in England had a surname.

Things were different in the other parts of the British Isles. In Wales, for instance, having a name derived from your ancestors was already in place, and well before 1066 everyone in the country would have had a name like Owen son of John. It was Henry VIII who decided that the Welsh should use the same system as the English. When he did so, many Welsh people needed a new surname, so they adapted their family names and added an 's'. Son of John became John's, or Jones. That explains why Jones is still one of the most popular surnames in Wales, along with Davies, Griffiths and Evans.

Why do church organs have multiple keyboards, and how does the organist know which one to use?

You might see two, three or four keyboards (called 'manuals') on an organ, but looking inside you would notice thousands of pipes, ranging from the size of a pen to over 10 metres tall. To play the instrument, you select a pipe by using keys on the manuals, as well as controls called 'stops', which change the pitch and volume of a note. You might play a C note on the keyboard, but the stops decide whether it will sound low, high, loud or soft.

The manuals control different groups of pipes. If an organ has two keyboards, they're likely to be the Great (which controls the boldest sounds) and the Swell (which activates pipes housed in a box with a shutter, so you can create a gradually increasing sound), but there could also be the Choir (used to accompany voices) and the Solo (which sounds like specific instruments in an orchestra, such as an oboe or an English horn).

There is also a pedal board that is played with your feet. Piano music has two staves: the treble clef for your right hand and bass clef for your left. Organ music often has a third stave which is just for your feet.

While the music may call for a specific manual, organists can select one that works better for their organ, since their instrument will often have been custom-made for the space it is played in.

If the player wishes to make the loudest possible noise, they activate every stop so that every note plays at once, and this is where we get the expression 'pulling out all the stops'.

Why are earwigs called 'earwigs', when they don't look like wigs or ears?

There is a persistent myth that earwigs can live in your ears and lay eggs in your brain. Thankfully, this is not true, but they *can* crawl into your ears, which seems to be where we get the word 'earwig' from. And it's not just an English phenomenon: in France, their name translates as 'ear piercer', while in Germany they are called 'ear worms'. Pliny the Elder recommended that if an earwig did get stuck in your ear, then the best way to remove it was to get someone to spit into your lughole. We don't recommend this.

The 'wig' part of its name comes from the word 'wicga' (meaning beetle, worm or insect), which is from the same root as 'wiggle'. The word tells us more about the movement of the creature than about its resemblance to a hairpiece.

Should you say 'wriggle room' or 'wiggle room'?
'Wiggle room' is the original and most widely used form, but those who prefer 'wriggle' tend not to take well to the idea that they should switch sides.

Do fish get seasick?

Flying fish do – by which we mean fish that are literally flying.

In 2009, a German scientist put 49 fish on a plane, which was then sent into a nosedive. He reported that immediately afterwards eight of the fish 'looked as if they were going to vomit' and noted that they were swimming in circles, doing somersaults and generally acting confused. He put it down to a kind of 'seasickness'. The motion, he said, had disrupted their balance, just as it does with humans on a boat. Though we can only speculate as to how much of the fishes' confusion came from the very fact of finding themselves on an aeroplane.

Why don't crocodiles have hair?

Because they're reptiles.

In the animal kingdom, all mammals have hair, including humans, cats, dogs and horses. Even dolphins are born with a tiny moustache. But there are no non-mammals with hair, although tarantulas have little bristles which look like – but, crucially, aren't – true hairs.

Crocodiles are reptiles, so instead of hair they have scales. These are useful because they're tough, which is good for defence, and they help to retain water, which is why reptiles can spend more time on land than scaleless amphibians.

There is one type of reptile that wears a wig, though. The Mary River turtle, which lives in Queensland, Australia, likes to cover itself with algae. Its bright green Mohican, which is made out of algae, has made it an online viral sensation, earning it the nickname 'the punk turtle'.

· ·SNAPPY SKILLS· ·

❯ Crocodiles can't grow hair, but they *can* gallop, climb trees, live for over a year without eating and dissolve bones with their stomach acid.

Why don't we say 'sheeps'?

. . . .

The answer to this question goes back a thousand years, to the earliest recorded form of our language, Old English.

Old English (OE) is very different to modern English and impossible to read without special study. Its words are largely based on Germanic ones, because Britons at the time had mostly come from Germanic areas. OE words that have survived into modern English are often nouns that were used by medieval Britons every day, such as 'house', 'hand', 'rat', 'egg' and (crucially for our question) 'sheep'.

The grammar of OE was much more complicated than the grammar taught in English lessons today. There were many ways of making plurals. For some words you added an '-en' at the end, while others ended with '-a', '-as' or even '-ru'. So, in the plural, the list of words above would become: *housen*, *handa*, *ratas* and *eggru*. Some words changed spelling completely in the plural (*book* became *beek*, for instance) and some didn't change at all: the OE for a sheep was *scēap*, and the basic plural form was *scēap* too.

So far, so complicated. But then 1066 happened.

Over the 100 years or so after the Norman Conquest, the Middle English (ME) period kicked off. Because the Normans had come from France, the English language became much more of a hybrid, with thousands of new words imported from over the Channel. French plurals are much simpler than Germanic ones: with a few exceptions, you simply add an '-s'. And so that became the standard way of writing a plural in English. 'House' in the plural became 'houses', and we could count the 'rats' and 'eggs' on our 'hands'.

But why isn't it 'sheeps'?

While the new '-s' ending became very common indeed, a word that was in constant use wasn't always updated. For instance, the standard OE '-en' ending survives today in the words 'children', 'brethren' and 'oxen', which are all very ancient words. This is also why we still say 'teeth' instead of the more logical 'tooths'.

Some ancient words, like 'sheep', never had a separate plural to change to the new French version. And that's why the plural of 'sheep' today is 'sheep'. The same happened with other OE words, including *deor* ('deer') or *swin* ('swine'), which were identical in the singular and the plural then as they still are today. Some linguists think this was particularly common with words for animals that were eaten, since they had a special cultural meaning to the Anglo-Saxons, but it's hard to prove that one way or the other.

Ultimately, this tangled history shows that languages are a huge hotchpotch of different influences over many centuries. 'Sheep' are still 'sheep' thanks to a little bit of chance. Ironically, it's one of the words that didn't follow the rest of the flock.

What do you get if you cross a sheep with a kangaroo?

....

A woolly jumper.

Not really. It's not possible for sheep and kangaroos to cross-breed, but you might be surprised by which creatures can.

You probably learnt at school that the definition of a species is a group of similar organisms that can breed with one another to produce fertile offspring. All types of dog can reproduce with one another, and their children and grandchildren can do the same, because they're all the same species. A horse and a donkey are related species that can procreate to have a mule, but the mule will be infertile and unable to have children of its own. '*Cum mula peperit*' was an expression used in ancient Rome that translates as 'when a mule gives birth'. It was the Roman equivalent of 'when pigs fly'.

But sometimes pigs *do* travel in aeroplanes and mules *do* give birth. There have been around 60 reported cases of mules having offspring, with one in 2007 that was verified through genetic testing. Ligers and tigons are cross-breeds between lions and tigers that often produce fertile offspring. Our ancestors even gave interspecies breeding a go, with the latest studies showing that *Homo sapiens* had fertile children with both Neanderthals and Denisovans. Your school textbook's definition of a species might need some updating.

More imaginative and unexpected cross-breeds may yet occur in our lifetime. In 1998, scientists in Dubai thought it would be useful to have an animal with the strength of a camel and the long hair of a llama, so they made a cama. At the time of writing, no one has tried to create a cama-chameleon.

Who came up with the phrase

 'Once upon a time'?

Once upon a time there was a mythical knight called Sir Ferumbras. He was the sultan of Babylon's son, stood over four metres tall (according to some accounts) and was famous for pillaging Rome. But, even more importantly, a telling of his story from the year 1380 begins with 'Onys . . . oppon a day', which the *Oxford English Dictionary* cites as the earliest version of the classic fairy-tale introduction.

The phrase became a storytelling staple. By 1632, it was already a cliché, with the 17th-century dramatist Thomas Dekker writing, 'Cannot you begin a tale to her, with once upon a time . . .'

Almost every language has its own version. In Latvian it's 'Once long ago in times long gone . . .', in Czech it's 'Beyond seven mountain ranges, beyond seven rivers . . .', and the Koreans say, 'When tigers used to smoke . . .'

What about 'happily ever after'?

The use of 'happily ever after' to mean married bliss originated in the early 18th century. The first written English example comes from the translation of an Italian work in 1702, which ends with the line (spoiler alert) 'Paganino, hearing the News, married the Widow, and as they were very well acquainted, so they lived very lovingly, and happily, ever after.'

Again, each country has its own take on the phrase. In

Spanish there is 'They were happy and ate partridges', while Icelandic stories end with the slightly more blunt 'A cat in a bog arched its back, the fairy tale is now over.'

Why do the characters always live happily ever after?

The idea of a 'fairy-tale ending' is fairly modern. Folk tales didn't always finish so happily. In a Victorian version of 'The Story of the Three Bears', it's an old woman, not Goldilocks, who trespasses. To punish her for breaking and entering, the bears try to burn and then drown her, until finally she is impaled on the top of St Paul's Cathedral (presumably the Tower of London was too spiky and the Royal Albert Hall not spiky enough). In Hans Christian Andersen's original version of 'The Little Mermaid', the title character dissolves into foam when she breaks her promise to the sea witch.

The Brothers Grimm are the most famous tellers of fairy tales, but their original collections were aimed at adults, not children, and the stories certainly reflect that. In 'Cinderella', one sister tries to force her foot into the slipper by chopping off her big toe. In 'Snow White', the queen attends the wedding between Snow White and the prince, where she is made to dance in red-hot iron shoes until she drops dead. And the tale 'The Death of the Little Hen' ends simply with 'and then everyone was dead'.

· FAIRY DUST ·

❯ In 2015, a scientific study worked out how practical Cinderella's glass slippers would have been, finding that if she'd tried to run, they would have shattered immediately.

Why are booby traps called 'booby traps'?

Since the 16th century, a 'booby' has meant somebody who's childish or foolish. A booby trap was originally a method of catching out a fool, and the name stuck.

'Booby' has also been used in the US to mean a type of horse-drawn sleigh ('Two elegant new boobies, nearly finished'), in Australia as slang for a prison ('She gets three months in the booby'), and, of course, there's the booby prize – a joke gift for coming last in a competition.

Then we have the boobies, a family of tropical seabirds that includes the blue-footed booby, the red-footed booby and the masked booby. Male boobies perform elaborate dances to find a mate, and they defend their territory by doing lots of head-nodding and prodding. The birds were so named for their supposed lack of intelligence, as they were unafraid of humans and so easily captured and killed. The dodo was similarly nicknamed (after the Portuguese word *doudo*, meaning 'fool'), but unlike the dodo, boobies are still around today, so perhaps a rebrand is in order.

If Rome wasn't built in a day, how long did it take?

....

The phrase 'Rome wasn't built in a day', referring to ancient Rome, was first written down, in French, in 1190.

For a more accurate estimate of how long it *did* take, we need to establish when building work began. This is hard, precisely because there's so much history there. Archaeologists are reluctant to dig up, for instance, the Colosseum or the Sistine Chapel in the hope of finding a chunk of Bronze Age wall underneath. But they did recently drill boreholes under a 15th-century church and uncovered evidence that people lived in Rome 3,500 years ago, so we know building work had begun by 1500 BC.

Rome was no more than a small village at that time. The date of its inception as a city is usually given as 21 April 753 BC. It took the ancient Romans many centuries to agree on this, but in the 1st century BC a scholar called Varro estimated a year-by-year chronology by counting back through all the consuls, wars and other historic events. 753 BC, he concluded, was the year that the twins Romulus and Remus founded the city. According to Roman mythology, they chose the spot where a wolf had rescued them as babies and suckled them to health, with the help of a woodpecker who brought them food.

Hardly any of the original city remains today. The longest-lasting, most impressive buildings began to appear from 200 BC, their longevity in large part down to one of the Romans' most extraordinary innovations: concrete. Engineers have studied Roman concrete for centuries, as it's more durable than the version we use today and actually gets stronger over time. One of the secrets to its longevity is the volcanic ash – or 'tuff' – that was mixed into it. It was used to build bath houses, theatres, circuses, the Colosseum and the Pantheon. In fact, the Pantheon's dome remains the largest unreinforced concrete dome in the world.

So we have three possible dates on which building may have begun: 1500 BC, 753 BC and 200 BC. As to when construction finished, the official date for the fall of Rome is usually given as AD 476, when the last emperor – who, like the first, was called Romulus – was deposed by a barbarian. But the city had passed its peak by that point. The last great temple to be constructed was the Temple of Saturn, rebuilt in around AD 370 after a fire. By our calculations, this means ancient Rome took either 570, 676, 1,123, 1,229, 1,870 or 1,976 years to build, depending on your interpretation. Perhaps this is why people dodge the question and refer to it as the Eternal City.

· **SOME ROME TRUTHS** ·

❯ From 800 to 1349, the Colosseum was rented out as apartments.

❯ When the Vandals sacked Rome in AD 455, they explicitly avoided committing vandalism. They made an agreement with the Pope to take the money but not to damage any property.

❯ The Romans created the first road signs. Most told you how many miles you were from Rome, as well as who was in charge of repairs for that area.

❯ Roman general Pompey tried to celebrate a victory by riding an elephant-drawn chariot through Rome, but gave up after the elephants got stuck in the city gate.

How wide are the borders between countries?

. . . .

Most national borders have no width. They are invisible, theoretical divisions, meaning that the moment you leave one country, you immediately enter another. Many of them haven't been around for long: a third of the world's borders are less than a century old.

Physical borders, with a measurable width, are becoming much more common, though. For example, at the end of the Second World War there were just seven physical border fences or walls on Earth; today, there are more than 70.

Countries that mark their borders do so in a number of ways:

. . . .

The Netherlands and Belgium

During the First World War, Germany installed the 'Wire of Death' on Belgium's northern border to prevent people fleeing the newly occupied territory. In spite of its lethal voltage, many still tried to cross it and escape to the Netherlands. An estimated 2,000–3,000 people died by electrocution, though there were a few successful attempts, including at least one person who pole-vaulted over.

Today, the border is open and much more welcoming. The Dutch town of Baarle-Nassau, which entirely surrounds small patches of Belgian territory, marks the national boundary with white crosses that have 'NL' written on one side and 'B' on the other. Restaurants and bars straddle the border, meaning you might be eating in Belgium, while your companion sitting opposite dines in the Netherlands.

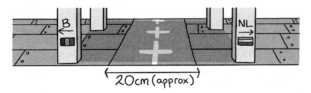

20cm (approx)

The US and Mexico

More than half the length of the US–Mexico border is water. In the 1840s, the two countries decided the Rio Grande river would be the dividing line between Texas and Mexico. The problem was that rivers – unlike walls and fences – move of their own accord. After heavy storms in 1864, the Rio Grande burst its banks. By the time the floods had receded, the main channel had moved south, effectively transferring 700 acres of land from Mexico to Texas. This tiny patch of floodplain was named the Chamizal, after a plant that grows there. It caused such a bitter dispute that the first-ever meeting between a US and a Mexican president was organised in 1909 to resolve it – at which someone attempted to assassinate both of them.

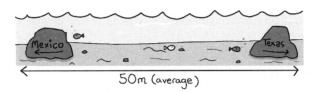

50m (average)

North and South Korea

The Korean Demilitarised Zone, the buffer between North and South Korea, is one of the only borders in the world to consist of an effective no-man's-land. It's flanked by two of the most militarised strips of land on Earth, as each country defends its own side. When the people of one country want to communicate with the other, they fly helium balloons over it or broadcast announcements via loudspeaker. Usually, these are straightforward propaganda messages, but South Koreans have also flown balloons carrying dollar bills and chocolate bars into the North.

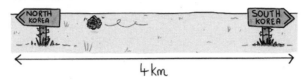

India and Pakistan

The 3,300 km border between India and Pakistan has a very physical presence. Beside the rows of high barbed-wire fence that run along it, India has installed floodlights. This makes it the only international border that astronauts can clearly see from the International Space Station at night.

Every day at sunset, Indians and Pakistanis perform a military ceremony at the main road crossing between their countries – the Wagah–Attari border. The gate is opened, and soldiers from each country march towards it, flinging their legs above their heads. Once they meet in the middle, they exchange a firm handshake, beat a retreat and compete to see who can lower their flag fastest. Soldiers involved in the ceremony get paid extra for maintaining an elaborate moustache and beard.

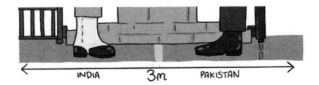

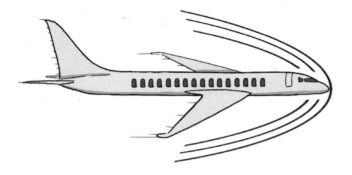

Which commercial airliner
first broke the sound barrier?

In December 1968, two months before Concorde's maiden flight, the Soviet Union unveiled a commercial supersonic airliner, the Tupolev TU-144. It wasn't so much a triumph of engineering as one of industrial espionage: they had based it on documents relating to Concorde that were leaked by a British engineer.

But the Soviets had to cut corners in order to beat the West to it. Seating on the plane was cramped, tray tables stuck, window blinds fell open without warning, and the toilets were often out of order. Unlike Concorde, the TU-144 couldn't cruise at supersonic speeds, so its afterburners (components that inject thrust) were constantly firing. This, combined with a primitive air-conditioning system, caused a deafening racket onboard, and passengers could communicate with each other solely by passing written notes.

The plane used so much fuel that it could only just make the journey from Moscow to Kazakhstan's capital, Almaty, a distance of about 3,000 km (similar to flying from London to Athens, and less than two-thirds of the distance from London to New York). It was cheaper than Concorde, though, with subsidised tickets costing just 37 roubles – the same price as any other comparable flight.

For just over two years, the TU-144 flew weekly on its only designated route – from Moscow to Almaty – during which time it suffered 226 mechanical failures. In 1973, one of the planes crashed during a demonstration at the Paris Air Show and 14 people were killed. The USSR continued to use TU-144s to train pilots, and NASA borrowed one in the 1990s for supersonic research, but by that time its days as a commercial airliner were over.

What causes that beautiful smell after rain?

There's a family of bacteria called *Streptomyces*, which live in soil all over the world. They get their energy from decaying vegetation and produce a chemical called geosmin, which gives soil its earthy smell. When raindrops hit the ground, tiny droplets of geosmin can fly up into the air and sometimes reach our noses. That's the main element of what we're smelling after a rainstorm – but it's not aimed at us.

The smell of geosmin is also extremely attractive to tiny, one-millimetre-long creatures called springtails. Whenever a springtail senses the chemical, it comes to eat the bacteria that produced it. This means the springtail gets a free meal, but the bacteria get something too. *Streptomyces* make spores, just like mushrooms, which they use to reproduce. When the hungry springtail turns up, the spores of the bacteria stick to it, and future generations of bacteria are carried to a whole new area where there might be plenty of fresh rotten vegetation to eat. Geosmin also repels fruit flies, so the bacteria have less competition for their food.

Humans are very sensitive to the smell of geosmin. In fact, we can detect it in concentrations as low as 100 parts per trillion, meaning we're 10,000 times more sensitive to it than sharks are to blood. There's no definitive answer as to why we like the smell so much, but some experts think we might associate the smell of rain with new growth, new life and new things to eat.

The smell created by geosmin is known as petrichor. It sounds ancient but was actually coined in 1964 by the Australian scientists who first properly studied it, Isabel Joy Bear and Richard Thomas. It comes from two Greek words: *petros*, meaning 'stone', and *ichor*, a mythical word for 'the blood of the gods'.

. . . .

Is there a smell that comes *before* a storm?

There is. It's the smell produced by molecules that have been formed by lightning. The heat from a bolt causes nitrogen and oxygen atoms to come together to make nitrous oxide (also known as laughing gas), but that often results in spare oxygen atoms floating around. These can re-form in triplets – O_3, which is a gas called ozone. As a thunderstorm approaches, the advance draughts of ozone mean you can smell it coming – hopefully allowing you to find somewhere to shelter before the heavens open.

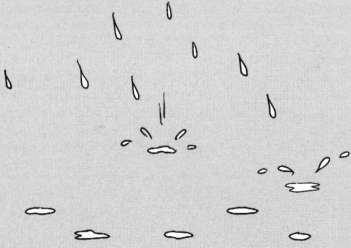

Why do some plants close their flowers at night?

They might add some colour to your garden or look good in a vase, but a flower's primary purpose is to help create new plants. A plant's reproductive system is found at the base of its petals, and since they can't walk around looking for a mate, they rely on passing insects, who are attracted to a flower's scent and appearance, to pick up and transfer pollen and seeds to help the plant reproduce.

But there are risks in keeping your reproductive parts exposed to the elements. Wind and rain can damage them, and passing animals might eat them. Since most pollinating insects only come out during the day, there's no reason to keep the shop open after hours, so some flowers lock themselves up every evening. Scientists think that the flowers respond to the drop in temperature at sunset and the gradual warming the next morning.

What is the most dangerous plant?

There are several contenders. Giant hogweed (*Heracleum mantegazzianum*) is often named 'Britain's most dangerous plant' as its toxic sap can cause burns when in contact with human skin. In Australia and Asia, you should watch out for the jequirity bean (*Abrus precatorius*, also known as 'rosary peas'). The seeds are safe to handle if they're intact, but if scratched or broken, they can kill you. They are used in jewellery-making, presumably by craftspeople who have nerves of steel. And in North America, the most toxic plant is water hemlock (*Cicuta maculata*). Despite its fearsome reputation, the roots of the plant look a lot like a harmless parsnip, and apparently it also tastes of parsnip . . . before it kills you. The plant can also be found in the UK, and in 2017, North Ayrshire council issued a warning about 'poisonous parsnips' washing up on local beaches.

Water hemlock is closely related to poison hemlock (*Conium maculatum*), which is native to Europe. The plant was most famously used to execute Socrates in AD 399 for the crime of 'corrupting the young'. After he was convicted, Socrates was asked to suggest his own penalty – common practice for defendants at the time. He replied that he shouldn't be punished at all but rewarded with free meals for life. The jury declined, and his 'final meal' was administered as a cup of poisonous tea.

The ancient Greeks also grew deadly nightshade (*Atropa belladonna*). Every part of this plant is poisonous, but it didn't stop women from using extract of 'belladonna' as eye drops to dilate the user's pupils. Definitely don't try this at home, as other side effects include sweating, vomiting, hallucinations and potentially death.

Which lottery numbers should I pick?

The real question is: which numbers *shouldn't* you pick? If you win the lottery with a common selection, such as 1, 2, 3, 4, 5, 6, then you'll have to share the prize with more people, so start by ruling out the most common choices.

In the UK, the most popular numbers for Lotto players are multiples of seven: 7, 14, 21, 28, 35 and 42. The second most common selection is multiples of five – 5, 10, 15, 25, 30, and 35 – while hundreds of players choose 4, 8, 15, 16, 23 and 42: these were the winning lottery numbers of the character Hurley in the TV series *Lost*.

Picking numbers associated with special dates might seem like a good start, but you run the risk that they won't be unique. Two players in Ireland once had to split the lottery jackpot because they both picked digits based on the birth, ordination and death dates of the same priest.

To make it less likely that you'd have to share any winnings, your best bet is to choose your numbers at random. You should discard and redraw them if they have any obvious pattern (i.e. 10, 12, 14, 16, 18 and 20), if they're all clustered together, or if they make a pattern when marked on the lottery ticket (such as a diagonal or vertical line).

The real way to avoid making a loss might be not to play the lottery at all. In the year ending March 2020, about 57% of money raised from ticket sales went into prizes, meaning there's an average payout of 57p for every £1 spent.

Okay, what other types of lottery can I play?
Some countries, including Taiwan, the Czech Republic and Lithuania, have run schemes in which shopping receipts count as lottery tickets. This makes it harder for companies to avoid tax, because everyone becomes desperate for a receipt, which creates a paper trail of their takings. Other lotteries that have been trialled include a Swedish anti-speeding lottery, where if a speed camera spotted you driving under the speed limit, you were entered into a draw, and a Taiwanese dog-poo lottery, where one bag of droppings equalled one chance to win.

.... **BONUS BALLS** ....

> In December 2020, the winning numbers for the South African national lottery were 5, 6, 7, 8, 9 and 10.

> In 2016, an Illinois man named Larry Gambles won his second major lottery prize.

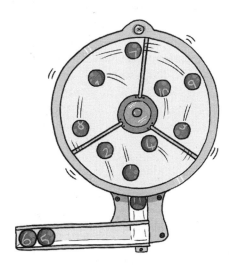

How do you keep Prosecco fizzy?

On the rare occasions when there's Prosecco left in the bottle, it's crucial to know the best way to keep your bubbly bubbly, and thankfully it's a problem that academics have devoted time to solving.

In 1994, a Stanford University chemist set up an experiment involving 10 identical bottles. As far as we know, they were neither green nor hanging on a wall, but they did each contain sparkling wine. He recruited a team of tasters, poured a glass from each bottle, then tried various sparkle-saving methods, including recorking, chilling the bottles and placing both silver and stainless-steel spoons in the neck. After 26 hours, they returned and compared the previously opened bottles with a freshly popped one in a blind taste test, and the results were surprising: simply chilling the leftover sparkling wine produced the fizziest drink of all; some of the team even thought it was fizzier than the bottle they had just opened.

So the best place for your leftover Prosecco is in the fridge, and the best place for your spoons is in the cutlery drawer.

How much sugar can you fit in a cup of tea?

When you add sugar to your tea, the liquid breaks it down into tiny pieces, which then find their way into the gaps between the tea molecules. It looks like the sugar has disappeared, but it's actually just very tiny and hidden. There are only so many hiding places, though, so at a certain point there will be no more gaps for the sugar to find. At that moment, your tea is 'saturated' with sugar.

For a small cup of tea, that level of saturation will occur after about 150 teaspoons. Beyond that point, you could add more, but the sugar would retain its crystal form and give your tea an unpleasant grainy texture. By then, it would be so sweet that you probably wouldn't want to drink it anyway.

How do I remove permanent marker from a whiteboard?

If you've picked up the wrong pen and accidentally scrawled on a whiteboard with a permanent marker, don't worry – there is a solution.

Permanent markers and whiteboard pens work in a similar way and consist of three key elements: a colorant, a solvent and a resin. The colorant is the pigment which gives the pen its colour. By itself, it usually takes the form of a fine powder; in a pen, it is dissolved in the liquid solvent – usually an alcohol such as ethanol – so that it can flow out and you can write with it. Then there's the resin, which is basically glue.

When you write, all three substances are transferred from inside the pen to the surface you are writing on. The invisible solvent quickly evaporates, leaving behind the visible colorant and the resin. The resin then dries, gluing the colorant to the surface.

The big difference between permanent and non-permanent markers is the resin. Whiteboard pens use a resin that can be broken apart by wiping it with a cloth or washing it off with water. Permanent-marker resin is stronger and needs to be dissolved in order to be removed. Household items like hand sanitiser or nail-varnish remover will do the trick, but if you're next to a whiteboard, the chances are that the closest source of solvent is actually a normal whiteboard marker. If you can quickly trace over the permanent pen's writing with the marker, the new layer of solvent will dissolve the resin, meaning you can simply wipe away all the marks in one go. It's ideal for quick fixes if a teacher is just around the corner . . .

Why do you hardly ever see £50 notes?

In 2021, there were 4 billion banknotes in circulation in the UK. Less than 10% – around 357 million – were £50 notes. 357 million is still quite a lot, but fifties don't get around nearly as much as other denominations. There are only slightly more £5 notes than there are fifties, but YouGov found that one-third of people surveyed had never owned a £50 note. They are rarely used in day-to-day transactions, and many cash dispensers don't hold them.

One reason for this is that high-value notes are often used in criminal activity. £10,000 in £50 notes is much easier to carry than the same amount in fivers, so they're perfect for a quick, illicit exchange of illegal goods for money. They can also help people evade tax: if someone does a high-value job and it's paid for in cash, there's no electronic record of the transaction, so it can be hidden from the taxman.

In 2016, economist and senior banker Peter Sands wrote a report saying that high-value banknotes 'play little role in the functioning of the legitimate economy, yet a crucial role in the underground economy'.

The eurozone has an even more valuable note worth €500 (about £430). They stopped printing these notes in 2019, but existing ones are still in circulation, which means criminals can still take advantage of them. In 2010, the UK's Serious Organised Crime Agency (now the National Crime Agency) reported that 90% of the €500 notes issued in the UK were held by criminals, with just 10% being used for travel and tourism.

When a competition offers a prize of a lifetime supply of something, what constitutes a lifetime supply?

There's no absolute answer to this, so it's always worth checking the Terms and Conditions. Most companies will do some research in advance to work out how much chocolate, say, the average person gets through over a lifetime; they need to be confident that if the winner is unhappy with their prize, the complaint won't be upheld by the Advertising Standards Authority.

Often the winner will receive a book of vouchers that allows them to collect the goods at their leisure, but it doesn't always work that way. In 2014, Californian Frank Cazares created a wedding dress from toilet paper for a competition and won a lifetime supply of toilet rolls. He was invited to a warehouse, where he was presented with a crate of 400 rolls. Then, every couple of months a truck would pull up outside his house to deliver hundreds more. The rolls filled his garage, then his flat, so he started to make furniture out of them and gave them out as birthday and Christmas presents. But then the deliveries stopped. The company had worked out how many toilet rolls a man in his twenties would be expected to get through in his lifetime, and then simply shipped them as quickly as possible. Frank had been so generous that his supplies ran out three years later, in 2017.

Not everyone cleans up. One Canadian competition asked players to guess how many sheets of paper they thought a knife could cut through. The winner won a lifetime supply of knives, but since they had a lifetime guarantee, the prize was only one knife. In fairness, the company did replace a broken knife three times but refused after the fourth.

· · · · · · · · · · · · · · · · · **A PLACE ON THE KNOW-DIUM** · · · · · · · · · · · · · · · ·

> In 1912, the government of Toronto ran a fly-swatting competition. It was won by a 15-year-old girl who killed over half a million flies.

> Every year, Katmai National Park in Alaska holds Fat Bear Week – a competition to find the bear that has added the most weight in preparation for hibernation.

> Between 1912 to 1948, when art competitions were a part of the Olympic Games, three sculptors received Olympic medals for making medals.

> A country's birth rate typically drops nine months after its football team does well in an international competition.

What is the most expensive thing on Earth?

The costliest object ever constructed by humans is the International Space Station. It took 15 nations over 30 years to build, and factoring in the processes of development, manufacturing, transportation and assembly in space, its estimated total cost was $110 billion.

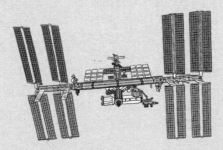

But *technically* it's not on Earth, so that's not the answer to this question.

The most valuable substance ever created is antimatter. This was discovered in the 1950s and can be thought of as the mysterious 'twin' particles of all the matter in the universe. Every particle has one of these twins, which is the same size but has the opposite charge. For instance, the electron, which is a simple negatively charged particle, has a twin called a positron, which is almost identical but is positively charged. Scientists theorise that the Big Bang created an antiparticle to match every particle, but they're not quite sure what happened to all the antiparticles. Only a few have ever been found.

They are even harder to create than to find. NASA's most recent estimated price for manufacturing a gram of antihydrogen in a particle accelerator is $62.5 trillion – three times the annual GDP of the US. Worse still, antimatter has a tendency to disappear as soon as you make it. The longest we've ever been able to keep hold of some is 405 days, so while it's the most expensive thing on Earth, it's not the most expensive thing for very long.

The most valuable long-lived object by weight and size is a single One-Cent Magenta stamp from British Guiana. It is the last-known surviving example of a special set that was printed in 1856, during a stamp shortage in the colony. It has a fascinating and chequered past, having bounced around the world from museums to private collectors, passing between 12-year-old stamp collectors, millionaires and even murderers. The blood-red stamp, which weighs only a fraction of a gram, sold at auction in 2014 for $9.5 million – that's more than a billion times its original value. Stamp collectors have declared it 'the *Mona Lisa* of philately'.

Incidentally, the actual *Mona Lisa*, which resides in the Louvre museum in Paris, was last valued by insurers in the 1960s at $100 million. Today, it's probably worth around $800 million, but even if you won the lottery every week for a lifetime, you still wouldn't be able to buy it since French law prohibits its sale.

The most expensive painting ever sold at public auction is the *Salvator Mundi*, a painting of Christ by Leonardo da Vinci, which was bought by a Saudi prince in 2017 for $450.3 million. However, rumours about its authenticity continue to circulate, and if it's not a real da Vinci, it will be worth a whole lot less. And that's the nub of it really – how much an item is worth really only depends on how much people are willing to pay for it.

How many items are there in the world?

. . . .

At least seven.

As I look around my elf-desk, I can see scissors, some sticky tape, a laptop, a glass of water, pens (all different, but all still pens), a copy of our last book, *Funny You Should Ask . . .*, and a biscuit. That's a good start – there must be at least seven objects there. But hang on, I've just taken a bite of my biscuit and a crumb has fallen off. Now I suppose that's eight things.

But what if I split a chunk off my biscuit and put it on the desk? 'Crumb' is a different word to 'chunk', so we could probably declare it another object. So with some manipulation I've managed to turn my biscuit into three separate objects – the crumb, the chunk and the rest. What if I attach the biscuit to my laptop with the sticky tape? Have I made a new item? Or combined three of them into one, causing the number to drop? It's already getting a bit tricky.

Of course, everything on my desk is made of atoms. There are 118 types of atom in the periodic table, and atoms themselves are made up of smaller items, such as protons, neutrons and electrons. The harder you look, the more things you find.

Once you get down to it, the smallest distance measurable, according to our current laws of physics, is a Planck length: 1.616255×10^{-35} metres. Nothing can be smaller than a Planck length, so if you divided the observable universe up into a three-dimensional grid of 'Planck cubes', you could safely provide an upper limit to the number of possible things in the universe.

The strange thing about mathematics is that if you have an upper limit to your problem, then you're halfway to solving it. And so we can say without a shadow of a doubt . . . that the number of items is between 10^{184} and seven.

. . . .

How many items are there *outside* the world?
Since the first spaceflights of the 1950s, humans have sent over 6,000 rockets into the sky, and many of their bits and pieces end up being discarded in orbit. Estimates suggest there are around 130 million man-made items in orbit around the Earth, a million of which are larger than a centimetre in width. This doesn't sound like much, but since the momentum of a grain of sand travelling at orbital speeds is enough to punch a hole in a satellite's hull, it's enough to give NASA's experts a severe headache.

Why are things interesting?

....

Hmm. Interesting question.

Many of the things that are most familiar to us – things we experience every day and take completely for granted – are, in fact, extremely, bottomlessly mysterious.

You may be surprised – and hopefully interested – to learn how many everyday concepts continue to baffle the finest human minds. Life, time, matter, mass, love, sleep, dreams, art, music, beauty, consciousness, gravity, laughter, ideas, language, numbers, emotions – there is no agreement, scientific or otherwise, on what any of these are, why they are there, or what they mean.

Philosophers and scientists cannot even agree on the meaning of the word 'meaning'. A book, a movie, a conversation, an insight – everyone recognises a meaningful experience when they have one, but no one can definitively say what that means.

Interestingness is another real head-scratcher. Some things are interesting, some aren't. Why? As far as we know, humans are one of the few species that are curious about stuff that doesn't affect their survival or the survival of their genes. Do leopards and spiders look up at the night sky and wonder what all the twinkly bits are?

Another puzzling idea – one that's very difficult to believe – is that curiosity may be a relatively recent phenomenon. Latin, for example, had no word for 'interesting'. Surely the Romans can't have been bored all the time? Conversely, the words 'bored', 'boring' and 'boredom' didn't exist in English until the 19th century. Is there something we haven't been told about Victorian England?

The watchword at QI is that everything in the universe, without exception, is interesting – if looked at for long enough, closely enough or from the right angle. In almost 20 years of trying, we've never found a subject of which this is untrue. But if we do eventually find one, we'll let you know.

Because that really would be quite interesting.

Answers to Eurovision question on page 42

'You're Not Alone', 'Go', 'Don't Play That Song Again', 'All',
'Rock Bottom', 'Come Back', 'That Sounds Good to Me',
'Only the Light', 'Even If', 'Congratulations'

Answers to Songs Stuck anagrams on page 156

Alan Davies, Zoe Ball, Sandi Toksvig

Credits

Publisher
Laura Hassan

Project Editor
Anne Owen

Editorial Assistant
Mo Hafeez

Copy-editor and typesetter
Ian Bahrami

Proofreader
Jodi Gray

Indexer
Mark Bolland

Art Direction
Donna Payne
Paddy Fox

Production
Pedro Nelson

Publicity
Rachel Alexander
Ruth Killick
Josh Smith
and Gaby Jerrard and Madelaine Bennett for QI

Marketing
John Grindrod
Jess Kim

Sales
Sara Talbot
Dave Woodhouse
Mallory Ladd

Audio
Catherine Daly

Legal
Suzanne King

Rights
Lizzie Bishop
Emma Cheshire

With Special Thanks to
Piers Fletcher, Dan Schreiber, Liz Townsend and the QI team

Al Booth, Ellie Caddell, Fiona Day, Hana Lockier, Ricky Marshall, James Santer, Helen Thomas and Mark Waring at the BBC

Meryl Hoffman and Callum Fosberry for Zoe Ball

Index

Michelangelo, 57
Middle English (language), 205
milk, 159
Ministry of Justice (UK), 174
Minkowski, Hermann, 192–3
Minogue, Kylie: 'I Just Can't Get You Out of My Head', 156
Mir space station, 64–5
Missouri, 120
mistletoe, 37
mitochondria, 96
mobile phones, 134
Mohican (hairstyle), 204
molecules, 23, 45, 50, 128, 146, 219, 225
moles (animal), 24–5
moles (espionage), 6
mollification, 175
Monet, Claude, 135
monkeys, 138
Montana, US, 120
Monty Python, 60, 199
Moon, 46–7, 146
moose, 73
Morse code, 87
Moscow, 217
mosquitoes, 130–1
motor racing, 111
Mötley Crüe, 92, 93
Motörhead, 92, 93
mountains, 50
mourning, 3
mouse (computer), 88
Mousetrap, The (play), 151
moustaches, 204, 215
Mud: 'Lonely This Christmas', 39
mules, 207
musculus complexus, 167

Museum of Hangovers, Zagreb 55
Museum of Natural History, Frankfurt, 143
museums, 136–7
music
  boy bands, 91
  Christmas, 38–9
  elephants' taste, 99
  Eurovision, 40–2
  organ, 201
myxozoans, 96

names/nicknames
  Big Apple, 120
  chess pieces, 144
  derby, 126
  long johns, 169
  'New' versions of European areas, 116–17
  operations, 9
  pasta, 18
  ships, 115
  US states, 120
Napoleon III, Emperor of the French, 22
NASA, 65, 217, 230–1, 235
National Grid, 82
NATO, 10–11
navigation, 4–5, 46
Neanderthals, 207
nerve compression, 157
nerves, 189
Netherlands, 14, 42, 116–17, 213
nettles, stinging, 171
neutrons, 234
New Caledonia, 116
New North Wales, 117

parking spaces, 145
Parmenides, 192
Parr, Catherine, 108
parsnips, 221
passport photos, 184
past, 192, 193
pasta, 18–19
pattern recognition, 75
pawns (chess), 144
pens, whiteboard, 226
Peppa Pig (TV show), 179
periodic table, 43, 234
permanent markers, 226
Peterson twins, 31
petrichor, 219
phonetic alphabets, 10
physics, 192, 234
pianos, 41
    literary, 86
    sheet music, 201
Piel Island (UK), 108–9
pigs, 68, 159, 174, 207
pins and needles, 157
pipes (organ), 201
placebo effect, 171
Planck length, 234
plants
    fruit, nut or vegetable?, 17–18
    most dangerous, 221
'Please do not touch' signs,
    136–7
Pliny the Elder, 37, 202
plurals, 205–6
plutonium, 59
pockets, 54–5
poison, 107, 127, 151, 153, 221
Poland, 29
pole-vaulting, 213
police, 6, 9, 57, 111

Polidori, John: *The Vampyre*,
    197
pollen, 104, 105, 173, 220
pollination, 67, 172, 173, 220
Pompey (Roman general), 212
poo, 37, 101, 175, 223
pork, 59
Portugal, 42
Portuguese (language), 210
positrons, 230
possibilism, 192, 193
potatoes, 55
pregnancy, 131, 173
present (time), 192, 193
presentism, 192
prisons, 210
prizes
    big apple, 120
    booby, 210
    funfair, 76–7
    lifetime supplies, 228–9
    lottery, 222, 223
    Rock, Paper, Scissors, 123
pronghorn, North American, 72
pronunciation
    Mötley Crüe, 92
    Shrewsbury, 85
propaganda, 214
proprioception, 189
Prosecco, 224
protons, 234
'p's, five, 157
psittacosaurus, 143
psychopathy, 132
puddings, 13
    plum, 32–3
'pulling out all the stops'
    (phrase), 201

quack doctors, 127
queens, types of, 108

racehorses, 9, 126
racewalking, 80
rain, 49, 218–19, 220
rainbows, 181
Ramon Berenguer II, Count of
    Barcelona, 106–7
Ramon Berenguer III, Count of
    Barcelona, 107
rams, 11
raspberries, 67
Raston, Colin, 164
rats, 46, 100, 158
rattlesnakes, Arizona, 162
reflexive awareness, 178
relativity, special theory of,
    192–3
remote cheering, 80
reptiles, 143, 204
resin, pen, 226
rheumatism, 55
rhinos, 73
rhymes, 3, 12, 34–5, 145
Richard, Cliff: 'Saviour's Day', 39
Rio Grande river, Mexico/US,
    214
road signs, 212
robotic diallers, 155
robots, 122
Rock, Paper, Scissors, 122–3
rockets, 235
Rockwell, Albert, 118
Rogan, John, 169
Rome, ancient, 9, 175, 207,
    211–12; see also Latin
'Rome wasn't built in a day'
    (phrase), 211

Romulus (last Roman emperor),
    212
Romulus and Remus, 211
rooks (chess), 144
Roosevelt, Franklin D., 121
roosters, 164
Royal College of Optometrists,
    139
Royal Household, 34
royal jelly, 104
Royal Navy, 113, 115
rugby league, 126
Russian (language), 144

Sacred Stones (company), 174
safe-cracking, 154–5
Sahara Desert, 4, 52–3
St Fiacre, 173
St Helens (rugby league), 126
St Paul's Cathedral, 209
salespeople, 194
salmon, 96
sand
    castles, 182–3
    grains at orbital speed, 235
    sculpture, 183
sand martins, 182–3
'Sandringham Time', 31
Sands, Peter, 227
sandwiches, 64, 65
Sardinia, 18–19
Saskatchewan, Canada, 79
satellites, 48, 235
saturation, 225
scales (reptiles), 162, 204
scent marking, 101
Scotland, 3, 12, 116
sculpture, 136–7, 183
seafood, 46

theft, 11, 54, 55, 57
Thiers, Jean-Baptiste, 95
Thomas, Richard, 219
thunderstorms, 49, 84, 219
tides, 46
tigers, 69, 207
tigons, 207
time
  daylight saving, 30–1
  dogs telling the, 75
  nature of, 192–3
  at Sandringham, 31
tin cans, 21, 142
tiptoe, walking on, 99
toads, 127
tobacco juice, 196
Todd, Prof. Gabrielle, 26
toenails, 138
toes, 138, 142
toilet rolls, 228
toilets, 83, 92, 216
Tokyo, University of, 122
tongues, 69
tongue-twisters, 190–1
toothpaste, 58
Toronto, Canada, 229
Tour de Donut, 15
trains, steam, 59
Transport for Greater
  Manchester, 162
trees
  Christmas, 35, 36
  crocodiles climb, 204
  felling on fingerprint island,
    57
  'Long John' nickname, 169
  mistletoe parasitism, 37
Triplaris trees, 169
tubed food, 58

tunnel-digging, 6
Tupolev TU-144, 216–17
turkeys, 165
Turner, J. M. W., 196–7;
  Chichester Canal, 196
turtle, Mary River, 204
Tutankhamun, 29
twins, 106–7
Tyndall, John, 45
typewriters, 86–7

Uber, 119
U-boats, 153
Uganda, 173
Ukraine, 35, 42
Ulm, University of, 4
umami, 13
umlauts, metal, 92, 93
underwear, 148, 169
United States
  burial guidelines, 174
  daylight saving time, 31
  ice-hockey violence, 124, 125
  Mexico border, 214
  operations, naming of, 9
  parking, 145
  passports, 184
  states' names, 120
  stockpiles, 59
up/down, 27
upset (emotion), 188
uric acid, 130
urine, 26, 146
USSR, 59, 124, 216–17
Utah, US, 120

Valentine, Dickie: 'Christmas
  Alphabet', 39
van Gogh, Vincent, 134